The Basics of the Christian Life

For which of you, intending to build a tower, sitteth not down first, and counteth the cost, whether he have sufficient to finish it?

LUKE 14:28

The Basics of the Christian Life

By

GEORGE SWEETING

MOODY PRESS
CHICAGO

If you enjoyed this course, you may want to consider studying one of the other Moody Press Electives.

Your Family, by John MacArthur, Jr.
Live Like a King, by Warren W. Wiersbe
Understanding Bible Doctrine, by
   Charles C. Ryrie

Copyright 1970, 1976, 1983 by
THE MOODY BIBLE INSTITUTE
OF CHICAGO

Second Revised Edition
Formerly titled *Living Stones*
ISBN 0-8024-0259-3
1 2 3 4 5 Printing/AF/Year 87 86 85 84 83

All rights reserved

Printed in the United States of America

CONTENTS

Chapter	Page
How to Use This Book	7
1. Your First Steps	9
2. What Is a Christian?	19
3. How to Grow in the Christian Life	32
4. You and the Holy Spirit	45
5. You and Your Bible	58
6. How to Pray	67
7. How to Have a Quiet Time	78
8. The Three Divisions of Mankind	92
9. How to Be Sure of Salvation	101
10. Worldliness and You	115
11. You and the Church	124
12. You and Your Money	134
13. Scripture Promises for Spiritual Problems	143

This book is affectionately dedicated to all my brothers and sisters of the Moody Bible Institute. Their partnership is a constant inspiration.

The heartbeat of our ministry at Moody Bible Institute is found in winning people to Jesus Christ and establishing them in their walk with God.

* * *

Sincere appreciation is extended to Miss Betty McIntyre for the hours of typing this and other manuscripts.

HOW TO USE THIS BOOK

1. *Read it alone.* Don't try to digest this material in one evening. Read a chapter a day. The important thing is to grasp it and apply it. Relate it to your job, your school, your family, and your church.

2. *Study it with someone else.* Secure another copy for a friend who recently has come to Christ. Spend a day or a night each week together.

3. *Use it in a group study—*
    a. as an elective in Sunday school
    b. in home Bible study
    c. as a Sunday evening training program elective
    d. for your instructional program for home visitation
    e. as a high school elective study course
    f. in follow-up classes for your camping programs for junior and senior high teens
    g. in adult vacation Bible school classes

These studies have been used by pastors all over the world in new-convert and church-membership classes. They have also been used in teenagers' meetings, in early morning men's and women's Bible study classes, and even in family devotions time.

There are many other ways to use this book; but, whatever way you choose, remember to
>> read it carefully,
>> read it prayerfully,
>> read it systematically,
>> and read it completely.

May God bless you as you go on in the Lord.

1
Your First Steps

For other foundation can no man lay than that is laid, which is Jesus Christ.

1 Corinthians 3:11

When by the Spirit of God, I understood these words, "The just shall live by faith," I felt born again like a new man: I entered through the open doors into the very Paradise of God!

Martin Luther

* * *

You, my friend, have taken a life-changing step. You have decided to begin a new life. God has become your heavenly Father and you are now His child; a wonderful eternal relationship has begun. It is really a brand-new beginning. In the words of Jesus, you have been "born again."

Possibly you feel very helpless to explain what has taken place. A new sense of freedom is yours. You are something like a happy child let loose in a big park. Practically everything is touched with divine newness and it is delicious. Do not be perplexed by what you have experienced, for this is wonderfully normal and right. The apostle Paul puts it this way, "Therefore if any man be in Christ, he is a new creature: old things are passed away; behold, all things are become new" (2 Corinthians 5:17). When you receive Jesus Christ, you become a brand-new person.

What You Have Done

1. You have acknowledged your need as a sinner.
What is the decision that you have made? You have acknowledged that you were wrong and God is right. You have agreed with God that you yourself are spiritually bankrupt. You have told the Lord of the poverty of your soul. Earnestly you have prayed, "God be merciful to me a sinner" (Luke 18:13). Your first step was to acknowledge your need as a sinner.

Dead and lost are the two Bible words used to describe your past life. Dead things cannot grow. You do not grow *into* grace; you grow once you are in it. Nothing is so completely helpless as that which is dead; and as far as God is concerned, all people through natural birth are spiritually dead. The Bible describes your spiritual transformation this way: "And you hath he quickened, who were dead in trespasses and sins" (Ephesians 2:1). Your life has been changed from a dead to a living state in Christ. God has touched your life and imparted divine life—His life—eternal life. This decision is really a death-breaking, earthshaking, heaven-awakening decision.

Lost is a descriptive word. The Bible states, "For the Son of man is come to seek and to save that which was lost" (Luke 19:10). Without Christ we are lost like sheep without a shepherd, helpless, hopeless, and defenseless. Lost, like the prodigal son, separated, destitute, and disgraced. By your decision you have been changed from a lost to a saved condition, changed from an enemy of God to a friend of God, changed from a stranger to a child of God. Your salvation is revolutionary.

Seneca, the philosopher, said, "We have all sinned, some more, some less."

Coleridge, the great thinker, confessed, "I am a fallen creature."

T. S. Eliot's character Cecilia Copplestone talks about her "awareness of solitude" and "a sense of sin."

The Chinese speak of "two good men: one dead, the other unborn."

The Bible plainly says, "For all have sinned, and come short of the glory of God" (Romans 3:23).

2. You have acknowledged Jesus Christ as your Savior.

The Lord Jesus Christ came into this world to meet our basic need. Christ was born to die. "This is a faithful saying, and worthy of all acceptation, that Christ Jesus came into the world to save sinners" (1 Timothy 1:15). This purpose was accomplished when He died on the cross. Repeatedly He told His disciples of His coming death. On the night of His betrayal by Judas, He broke bread with His disciples. Plainly He explained to them the purpose of the cross. "For this is my blood of the new testament, which is shed for many for the remission of sins" (Matthew 26:28). Paul simply and clearly wrote, "For he [God] hath made him to be sin for us, who knew no sin" (2 Corinthians 5:21).

Isaiah prophetically penned, "But he was wounded for our transgressions, he was bruised for our iniquities: the chastisement of our peace was upon him; and with his stripes we are healed" (Isaiah 53:5).

Our basic need is the forgiveness of sin. God's provision for our need is found in the death of Jesus Christ. Jesus Christ, the sinless Son, fully and completely bore the sins of the world. He took upon Himself our sin. The gospel is the good news of what God has done through Christ to forgive our sins.

Recognizing Christ as God's answer, that He died in your place, you have come asking for forgiveness of all your sins. "For Christ also hath once suffered for sins, the just for the unjust, that he might bring us to God" (1 Peter 3:18). In a definite act of faith, you have pledged your allegiance to Christ. At that moment, Jesus became your Savior, and God forgave your sins.

The word *confess* is an interesting word. It simply means to speak the same thing. It means to agree or acknowledge. You have first acknowledged your need as a sinner, but you have also acknowledged Jesus Christ as your personal Savior. What have you done? "Thou hast believed" (John 20:29).

3. *You are now beginning to acknowledge Jesus Christ before others.*

Your First Steps

You may ask, "Do I have to publicly confess Christ?"

I must answer, "Yes, Jesus Christ requests a public confession." And I might add, "How can you help it!"

Jesus plainly said, "Whosoever therefore shall confess me before men, him will I confess also before my Father which is in heaven" (Matthew 10:32). If you have sincerely trusted Christ, you will have to tell someone about it. This new life will be obvious, for "out of the abundance of the heart the mouth speaketh" (Matthew 12:34).

Some new Christians try to be "secret" believers, but this is unwise and wrong. Just imagine Dr. Jonas Salk keeping his polio vaccine a secret! This would have been criminal. So, too, a knowledge of God's salvation places us in debt to the whole world.

Both Nicodemus and Joseph of Arimathea tried to be secret disciples. It took the death of Christ to bring them to the place of openly begging for the body of Jesus from Pilate. The Scripture record is clear: "And after this Joseph of Arimathea, being a disciple of Jesus, but secretly for fear of the Jews, besought Pilate that he might take away the body of Jesus: and Pilate gave him leave. He came therefore, and took the body of Jesus. And there came also Nicodemus, which at the first came to Jesus by night, and brought a mixture of myrrh and aloes, about a hundred pound weight. Then took they the body of Jesus, and wound it in linen clothes with the spices, as the manner of the Jews is to bury" (John 19:38-40). Do not let your fear of others rob you of the joy of open allegiance. It is sin to be silent when to confess would help another.

To be ashamed of Christ is really a sad experience. It implies carelessness, error, and failure on our part. It dishonors Christ and brings personal defeat.

If Jesus Christ were ashamed of you and me, that we could easily understand; but for men and women to be ashamed of Christ is difficult to comprehend. Joseph Griggs asks,

> Jesus, and shall it ever be
> A mortal man ashamed of Thee?
> Ashamed of Thee, whom angels praise
> Whose glories shine thro' endless days?
>
> Ashamed of Jesus! Sooner far
> Let evening blush to own a star;
> He sheds the beams of light divine
> O'er this benighted soul of mine.
>
> Ashamed of Jesus! That dear friend
> On whom my hopes of heav'n depend!
> No, when I blush, be this my shame,
> That I no more revere His name.
>
> Ashamed of Jesus! Yes, I may,
> When I've no guilt to wash away;
> No tear to wipe, no good to crave,
> No fears to quell, no soul to save.

Ashamed of Christ? We must never be. Repeatedly we are encouraged in Scripture to confess Christ openly and not be ashamed. Jesus said, "Whosoever therefore shall be ashamed of me and of my words in this adulterous and sinful generation; of him also shall the Son of man be ashamed, when he cometh in the glory of his Father with the holy angels" (Mark 8:38). To be reproached for Christ now is to be rewarded later. At times we may be called upon to partake in Christ's sufferings. This really implies that He and we are together. "If any man suffer as a Christian, let him not be ashamed" (1 Peter 4:16), writes Peter.

I have found that failure to acknowledge Jesus Christ often results in careless living, but a public commitment puts one on record before God and man. The fact that others know of your decision will really help guard you against temptation.

Yes, your decision is a blessed one. With Philip Doddridge you can sing:

O happy day that fixed my choice
On Thee, my Saviour and my God.
Well may this glowing heart rejoice,
And tell its raptures all abroad.
Happy day, happy day,
When Jesus washed my sins away.

Yes, your decision has begun a real, happy, lasting change. You are ready to build a life for God.

What You Must Now Do

As a newborn baby is cared for in the physical world, you need to be helped spiritually. Let me list four helpful suggestions that I will enlarge upon in later chapters:

1. Read the Bible systematically.

What food is to the body, the Bible is to your new spiritual life. At a prescribed time, in a quiet place, each day should start with the Bible. This is a must if you are to grow in the things of God. The gospel of John is a good place for you to begin. Remember, at least a chapter a day! D. L. Moody said, "The Bible will keep you from sin or sin will keep you from the Bible." A chapter a day will certainly help to keep sin away.

2. Learn to pray.

Prayer is the communion of the believer with God; we speak to God, but He also speaks to us. Prayer is not merely asking favors of God, but rather waiting in quietness before Him. Pray for personal cleansing and victory over evil; pray for yourself and pray for others.

3. Use every opportunity to confess Christ before the world.

In a winsome way, immediately tell someone of your spiritual decision. Activity always strengthens. When believers share with others, they develop an appetite for Bible study. The result of their speaking to others of their new life will provide daily up-to-date subjects for prayer. When a new Christian begins working, everything comes into proper focus. R. A. Torrey said, "If you make but little of Christ, Christ will make but little of you."

4. Become part of a local church.

If a mother permits her children to grow up in idleness, the result will be untaught children. Since the Christian's responsibilities toward other believers is evident, waiting only forms bad habits. The Bible says, "Not forsaking the assembling of ourselves together, as the manner of some is" (Hebrews 10:25). Your faithful church attendance will help you in spiritual growth. Find a fellowship that gives full allegiance to Jesus Christ and the Word of God, and become part of it.

You will be sure to meet temptations, but you need not yield or fall, for God has promised, "Greater is he that is in you, than he that is in the world" (1 John 4:4). If you do fall, seek immediate forgiveness. "If we confess our sins, he is faithful and just to forgive us our sins, and to cleanse us from all unrighteousness" (1 John 1:9). If you fall, do not remain defeated, but get up and go right on. Perhaps right now you are facing the battle with some habit; remember that Christ is ready to help you, and He has all power in heaven and earth.

Another secret of victorious Christian living is to keep your eyes on Christ. The best of men will fail you at times, but never forget—Jesus never fails.

REMINDERS

Dead things cannot grow. You do not grow into grace; you grow once you are in it.

The Chinese speak of "two good men: one dead, the other unborn."

The gospel is the good news of what God has done through Christ to forgive our sins.

A knowledge of God's salvation places us in debt to the whole world.

"The Bible will keep you from sin or sin will keep you from the Bible," said D. L. Moody.

> "If you make a great deal of Christ, He will make a great deal of you; but if you make but little of Christ, Christ will make but little of you."
>
> R. A. TORREY

QUESTIONS

1. What is the first step in receiving Jesus Christ as Savior? *aknowledge sin*
2. Give two Bible words which describe our past sinful condition. *dead + lost*
3. What is the second step in receiving Jesus Christ as Savior? *acknowledge X*
4. What does the word *confess* mean? *acknowledge*
5. Give at least two verses of Scripture that indicate we should publicly confess Jesus Christ before men. *Matt 10:32, Matt 12:34*
6. List four important steps which will aid spiritual growth. *read Bible, Pray, Testimony, Church*
7. How have you acknowledged Christ before others? *yes*
8. Why are we sometimes ashamed of Christ?
9. Why is it important to attend church? To become a member? *Heb 10:25 Support*
10. What does God promise in 1 John 1:9 and 4:4? How can those promises be applied to our lives? *forgiveness of confessed sin / God is greater than world*

2
What Is a Christian?

> *But as many as received him, to them gave he power to become the sons of God, even to them that believe on his name: which were born, not of blood, nor of the will of the flesh, nor of the will of man, but of God.*
>
> JOHN 1:12-13

If we take the first three words of John 1:13 and the last two words, we have the phrase "which were born . . . of God." That's a good definition. A Christian is one who is born of God.

* * *

In scorn and ridicule the world gave birth to the word *Christian*. In Antioch of Syria, a city of a million inhabitants, the followers of Jesus were given this nickname. The word *Christian* appears only three times in the New Testament and never in the Old Testament. First in Acts 11:26: "And the disciples were called Christians first in Antioch." It appears again in Acts 26:28: "Then Agrippa said unto Paul, Almost thou persuadest me to be a Christian." And also in 1 Peter 4:16: "Yet if any man suffer as a Christian, let him not be ashamed; but let him glorify God on this behalf."

To be a Christian in the early centuries was a life-and-death proposition; it involved the faith of heroes. To be a Christian often meant facing a pagan arena and wild beasts; it *always meant* the narrow gate, the restricted way, the denial of self, shouldering a cross and following Jesus.

What Is a Christian?

1. To be united with Christ

The word *Christian* is really the combination of two words: *Christ* and *man*. When a man or woman is united with Christ, they form one word, *Christian*. A Christian is the combination of Christ and you. The sinner receives the Savior, and the Savior receives the sinner. A Christian is a Christ man or a Christ woman.

2. To be born again

When Jesus spoke to Nicodemus He said, "Except a man be born again, he cannot see the kingdom of God" (John 3:3). According to Jesus, a Christian is one who has been born again. Spiritual birth is the only way to enter God's family; we must be born again.

In our day, the word *Christian* has been seriously corrupted. It has been pulled and stretched to cover the whole civilized world. Often it has been misused, misapplied, misunderstood, and misappropriated. Thousands call themselves Christians who have no claim to the name at all. Some say, "All civilized people are Christians." Others suppose this word includes all Gentiles and excludes all Hebrews. To the contrary, there are many splendid people who are Jewish and Christian; and, sad to say, there are thousands of Gentiles who are not Christians at all. The concept of Christianity has become so distorted that millions do not know the difference between spiritual regeneration and mere religious profession.

The story is told of some American seamen marooned on a South Sea island. Fearing the natives, the sailors hid until one day they heard some of the inhabitants speaking perfect English. In relief, the marooned men exclaimed, "They are Christians!"

In reality, no one has the right in his unforgiven state to say, "I am a Christian."

You ask, "But why?" Because the Bible teaches that "all have sinned."

God's justice and holiness demand that sin be paid for and dealt with. Jesus, God's Son, voluntarily died to atone for the sins of all mankind. When one receives Christ in faith, then, *and only then*, does that one have the power or the legal right to be a child of God. John the apostle said, "But as many as received him, to them gave he power to become the sons of God, even to them that believe on his name" (John 1:12).

3. To receive Christ as Savior

To receive Christ is to have faith in Him, that He is the sinless Son of God, that He died voluntarily for our sins so that we might be free from spiritual death and judgment and have everlasting life. The all-important question is, Have you made this decision; have you received Jesus Christ?

A Word of Warning

Religion is quite popular in our day. The world is full of people who say, "I believe in God. I believe in Christ, and I believe in the Bible." Sometimes the lives of such people do not correspond with what they claim to believe. This is not a saving faith, but a false faith.

The Bible says, "Faith without works is dead" (James 2:20), and again, "By their fruits ye shall know them" (Matthew 7:20). So if there is no difference, no distinction, I fear that some individuals are in the flesh, and "shall of the flesh reap corruption" (Galatians 6:8).

You see, there is not a prisoner in the world who does not believe it is better to be honest. There is not a drunkard who does not believe it is better to be sober. But mere belief does nothing to change the condition. Faith has come to be thought of today as a simple acquiescence to the Word of God. But this kind of faith is paralyzing, deadening, and even damning. The Bible asserts, "The devils also believe, and tremble" (James 2:19). The difference between heart belief and head belief is the difference between salvation and damnation. Any faith that does not result in a changed life is not saving faith; it is a deceiving faith. So the important question to ask is, "Have I believed savingly?"

Occasionally there are those who claim they cannot believe what they do not understand. But in reality we believe much that we do not understand. For example, no one understands all the mysteries of electricity, yet it would be foolish to say, "I will sit in darkness until I understand electricity."

No doctor completely understands the marvels of the digestive system. Yet, who would say, "I will not eat until I understand the digestive system"?

Who understands the miracle of the common watermelon? A seed is dropped into the ground. It sprouts, and soon there is a vigorous plant which bears several watermelons, each of which is hundreds of times the weight of the original seed. Outside of each there is a beautiful coat of green, then a rind of white, and an enticing core of red with dozens of seeds, each capable of producing additional watermelons. The most brilliant man cannot explain this mystery, but the most ignorant man can enjoy it.

So when you submit to the gospel, you become part of the divine mystery. You are quickened by God and become "a new creature." Jesus said, "The wind bloweth where it listeth, and thou hearest the sound thereof, but canst not tell whence it cometh, and whither it goeth: so is every one that is born of the Spirit" (John 3:8).

By way of review:
1. A Christian is one who is united with Christ.

2. A Christian is one who has been born again.
3. A Christian is one who has received Jesus Christ.

What a Christian Is Not

Sometimes we understand the positive better by considering the negative. I remember well the happiness of my own boyhood experience. On Sunday, all six of us children accompanied Mother and Father to church; our meals were always prefaced with family prayer; we read the Bible systematically. Ours was a Christian home, yet this wonderful inheritance did not automatically make me a Christian. Relationship to the redeemed does not bring redemption. Kinship to Christians cannot make one a Christian. God's salvation is not by natural generation. God doesn't have any grandchildren. John 1:13 shares three errors that exist today. "Which were born, not of blood, nor of the will of the flesh, nor of the will of man, but of God."

1. Natural birth cannot make one a Christian.

". . . were born, not of blood."

John is simply saying that one does not become a Christian through our earthly parents. The blessing of a godly mother and a saintly father is a great heritage, but this does not make one a Christian. Parents can give a push in the right direction, but they cannot make us Christians.

The Jewish people used to say, "We have Abraham as our father," and therefore they thought they were safe and secure.

What Is a Christian?

The exponents of Nazism boasted of pure "Aryan blood" and talked of a "super race." This, too, is unscriptural. In the Bible the mystery of blood is in the heritage of sin, derived from Adam by natural birth. It is also in the gift of salvation purchased by the blood of Christ through spiritual birth. John the apostle is simply saying that one cannot become a Christian through earthly parents. Natural birth cannot make one a Christian.

2. Good works cannot make one a Christian.

". . . nor of the will of the flesh."

Probably the greatest error which exists today is the belief that salvation is the result of personal effort. Thousands imagine themselves Christian because they seek to keep the Golden Rule or because they live decent, moral lives. Some rely upon their religious activity or church membership. In direct contrast, the apostle John says that salvation does not come through "the will of the flesh."

I once asked a faithful church attender if she were a Christian. She quickly answered, "I have taught in the Sunday school for sixteen years."

I commended her and kindly repeated the question, "Are you a Christian?"

She then told me of her efforts in the missionary society, but did not answer my simple question. This dear lady was depending on her own efforts to earn salvation. If being active in religious work made one a Christian, she certainly would be one many times over; but the Bible says, "nor of the will of the flesh."

The Bible message is plain on this subject and easy to understand. Paul said, "For by grace are ye saved through faith; and that not of yourselves: it is the gift of God: not of works, lest any man should boast" (Ephesians 2:8-9). Salvation is not something you do, but Someone you receive. Salvation is Someone, Jesus Christ.

It would be easier to tunnel through the mountains with teaspoons than to get to heaven by personal effort, character, or morality. Salvation is an offer, not a demand. It is not based on what I do, but on what Jesus Christ has done.

We do not become Christians by climbing the ladder of good works, rung by rung. In fact, the very opposite is true. Jesus Christ came down the ladder via Bethlehem's manger and Calvary's cross to meet us where we are. Good works cannot make one a Christian.

3. *Religious ordinances cannot make one a Christian.*

". . . nor of the will of man."

Some time ago I asked a medical doctor, "Are you a Christian?" He answered, "I was baptized by Dr. So-and-so some years ago." After further discussion, I learned that he was banking everything on the ordinance of baptism rather than upon faith in Christ.

No man, no matter how prominent or how pious, can make you a Christian. The erroneous idea that some religious leader can make one a Christian by some religious act is untrue and contrary to the teaching of the Word of God. No church ordinance, however important, can forgive sin.

A tramp, obviously under the influence of alcohol, approached evangelist D. L. Moody. "Mr.

What Is a Christian?

Moody," he said, "you're the man who saved me."

As the great evangelist observed the bearded face, bloodshot eyes, unkempt hair, and torn clothes, he replied, "Yes, it looks as if I did save you. If the Lord had, you wouldn't be in this condition."

Ministers are instruments of God to perform His bidding. As Paul said, "We are labourers together with God" (1 Corinthians 3:9). "We are ambassadors for Christ, as though God did beseech you by us: we pray you in Christ's stead, be ye reconciled to God" (2 Corinthians 5:20). Never can any man confer salvation or forgiveness upon another.

Being a Christian is much more than believing certain doctrines or submitting to any ordinance. It is receiving Christ. If we take the first three words of John 1:13 and the last two words, we have the phrase "Which were born . . . of God." That's a good definition. A Christian is one who is born of God.

WHAT A CHRISTIAN OUGHT TO BE

For the apostle Paul, salvation and surrender were simultaneous. Immediately upon believing, he asked, "Lord, what wilt thou have me to do?" (Acts 9:6). Just as Paul wanted to do God's will only, so every Christian should commit his entire life to Christ. Paul called upon all Christians to "yield yourselves unto God" (Romans 6:13).

Adolph Deissman suggested that the word *Christian* means "slave of Christ," as *Caesarian* means "slave of Caesar."

In the Old Testament, God promised Abraham that he would be the father of a great nation, with children as numerous as the sand of the sea. But Abraham had no children. Contrary to the life of faith, he fathered a son by Hagar, his wife's slave. This act was of the flesh, representing man's blundering way rather than God's way. God intervened and performed a miracle. In her old age, Abraham's wife, Sarah, gave birth to Isaac, a child of faith, the fulfillment of God's eternal plan.

God calls each Christian to let go of his own solutions to life's problems and accept the way of faith. He is really saying, "Don't hang on to anything—*yield everything.*"

It is a big mistake to imagine you can carelessly ramble along in the Christian life. As Samuel Rutherford said, "You will not be carried to Heaven lying at ease upon a feather bed." Tertullian said, "He who fears to suffer cannot be His who suffered."

The call of Christ while on earth was uncompromising and unconventional. His words were so piercing that the hearers tried to kill Him. Yet, today, we often present the Lord of glory as meek and mild rather than high and holy, soft and sentimental instead of steadfast and strong. Artists and poets have portrayed Christ with flowing chestnut hair, a feminine face, going about breathing mild benedictions upon everyone. This is false! It is true that He went about doing good; but on the other hand, He was firm and His words were stringent. At times He gave offense to His disciples, to His relatives, to the scribes and Pharisees. On one occasion, Jesus said, "Think not that I am come to send peace on earth: I came not to send peace, but a sword" (Matthew 10:34).

True, He was loving and kind, but we must not overlook the demands of His call. "Lord," cried one man, "I will follow thee whithersoever thou goest."

Jesus answered the enthusiastic offer with a staggering response: "Foxes have holes, the birds of the air have nests; but the Son of man hath not where to lay his head."

Another cried, "Lord, suffer me first to go and bury my father."

The reply struck back as fast and devastating as lightning. "Let the dead bury their dead: but go thou and preach the kingdom of God" (Luke 9:57-60).

A third cried, "I will follow thee; but let me first go bid them farewell, which are at home at my house" (v. 61).

Jesus dealt a crushing blow when He said, "No man, having put his hand to the plough, and looking back, is fit for the kingdom of God" (v. 62).

The Christian life is beautiful but it is not a picnic. Jesus never gained disciples under false pretense. In fact, He never hid His scars, but rather declared, "Behold my hands and my feet" (Luke 24:39).

C. T. Studd's motto was, "If Jesus Christ be God and died for me, then no sacrifice can be too great for me to make for Him."

From history's pages we learn of a cowardly young soldier in the army of Alexander the Great.

Whenever the battle grew fierce, the young soldier would yield. The general's pride was cut because this timid soldier also bore the name Alexander. One day Alexander the Great sternly addressed him and said, "Stop being a coward or drop that good name."

The call to all Christians is the same today. May we faithfully live up to all the name Christian implies. "Lord, what will You have me to do?"

REMINDERS

A Christian is the combination of *Christ and you*.

Salvation is an *offer*, not a demand.

The difference between heart belief and head belief is the difference between salvation and damnation.

God doesn't have any grandchildren.

Jesus never gained disciples under *false pretense*. He never hid His scars, but rather declared, "Behold my hands and my feet."

"If Jesus Christ be God and died for me, then no sacrifice can be too great for me to make for Him."

C. T. STUDD

QUESTIONS

1. How many times does the word *Christian* appear in the Bible and where?

What Is a Christian? 31

2. Give two definitions in answer to the question "What is a Christian?" *plane to X/ Christ Man*
3. List three errors that exist, according to John 1:13. *not of blood, not of flesh, not of man*
4. According to John 1:12, what happens to the person who receives Jesus Christ? *right to become Children of God*
5. According to Acts 9:6, a Christian ought to be what? *surrender*
6. What did Paul call all Christians to do in Romans 6:13? *yield to God*
7. Why did Jesus use the words *born again* (John 3:3) to describe becoming a Christian? *new II Cor 5:17*
8. Why do some people think they are Christians when they are not? *Gentiles / misunderstand*
9. What is the "will of the flesh" (John 1:13)? Why is it insufficient for salvation? *good works*
10. As Christians, to what kind of life have we been called? *life of yielding + sacrifice*

3
How to Grow in the Christian Life

Building up yourselves on your most holy faith.
JUDE 20

How does the soul grow? Not all in a minute!
Now it may lose ground, and now it may win it;
Now it resolves, and again the will faileth;
Now it rejoiceth, and now it bewaileth;
Now its hopes fructify, then they are blighted;
Now it walks sullenly, now gropes benighted;
Fed by discouragements, taught by disaster;
So it goes forward, now slower, now faster,
Till all the pain is past, and failure made whole,
It is full grown, and the Lord rules the soul.

SUSAN COOLIDGE

* * *

Some time ago I read a book entitled *Grow Up or Blow Up*. The thrust of the book was that civilization must either grow up or else destroy itself. It is also very important that we as individuals "grow up" in the things of God.

How to Grow in the Christian Life

Our twentieth century finds the masses of people living and dying for material possessions. It appears that an unparalleled wealth fever afflicts the majority, while spiritual values are practically ignored. The true measure of success in life is not and cannot be counted in dollars and cents and surely not in physical or mental accomplishments. In complete contrast, the true and eternal measure of life is found in growth in a Christ-like character. You will find this road to be a neglected trail, because there are no superhighways to growth.

Robert Browning said, "Man was made to grow, not stop." The apostles Peter and Paul believed this truth too. Peter challenges all Christians to "grow in grace, and in the knowledge of our Lord and Saviour Jesus Christ" (2 Peter 3:18). The preceding verse contains a stern warning: "Beware lest ye also, being led away with the error of the wicked, fall from your own stedfastness." Immediately following the warning appears God's cure: "But grow in grace."

Romans 8:29 encourages every believer "to be *conformed* to the image of his Son." Ephesians 4:15 tells us to "*grow up* into him in all things." First Thessalonians 3:12 challenges us "to *increase* and abound."

LIFE: THE FIRST STEP OF GROWTH!

Dead things cannot grow. Before there can be spiritual growth, there must be spiritual life. When a child is born, his first cry indicates life. If there is life, then a world of possibilities beckons to this new baby. If there is *no life,* then there is *no hope.* A fence post placed in the ground will not grow, but a little seed will grow spontaneously. Drop a stone into the richest soil and it will be exactly the same size years later. Place a seed into the ground, and it will spring up and produce a stalk and flowers. The difference is plain: one has life while the other does not.

This divine life may be imitated, but the difference can be easily detected. One is real; the other is false. One is natural; the other is mechanical. The crystal grows from without by addition of new particles, while a living organism grows from within. The crystal may be beautiful, but it is only a crystal and lacks true life for growth. *Dead things may accumulate, but they cannot grow.* Unless men and women have the life that comes from above, religious practices and environment mean nothing. In fact, they cause a person to rest in a false hope, making condemnation more sure. To you who have made your decision for Christ, the divine command is "grow in grace." These to whom Peter is speaking have been "born again," for remember, dead things cannot grow.

The story is told of a young sixteenth-century artist who worked hard and long on a statue of an angel. The famous Michelangelo was invited to view the finished masterpiece. As Michelangelo gazed upon it, he commented, "It lacks only one thing," and then he left the studio.

The young artist was depressed as he wondered what his masterpiece lacked. A concerned mutual friend went to Michelangelo to discover what was missing. Michelangelo responded, "It lacks only one thing, and that is life. If it had life, it would be as perfect as God could make it."

Yes, *life* is the first requisite for growth.

WHY YOU MUST GROW

1. It is God's plan.

Second Peter 3:18 says, "Grow in grace, and in the knowledge of our Lord and Saviour Jesus Christ."

The Lord said to Moses and Aaron, "Ye shall therefore be holy, for I am holy" (Leviticus 11:45). Jesus also said, "Be ye therefore perfect [mature], even as your Father which is in heaven is perfect" (Matthew 5:48). Paul, speaking to the Philippians, said, "Not as though I had already attained, either were already perfect [full grown] . . . but this one thing I do, forgetting those things which are behind, and reaching forth unto those things which are before, I press toward the mark for the prize of the high calling of God in Christ Jesus" (Philippians 3:12-14). Paul was moving upward and onward.

Growth is not the dream of a starry-eyed idealist; it is God's intention. We must bend or be broken, for God will not tolerate continued interference. We are not sinless but we should sin less and less.

2. It is nature's law.

Nature says, "Grow or I will kill you." A cankered tree does not send forth new shoots. When the body stops growing it begins to die. The fingers of nature begin to pick and to pluck until death claims us. The first law of life is *expansion*. It is grow or decay! Advance or regress! Live or die!

Jesus said, "Every branch in me that beareth not fruit he taketh away: and every branch that beareth fruit, he purgeth it, that it may bring forth more fruit" (John 15:2).

"Grow in grace." The word *grow* denotes continuous action. There is no time to stop growing. If we do not grow in the physical realm, it is a sad sign; it is a mark of sickness. A mother would be justly alarmed if day after day and week after week her baby showed no signs of growth. A farmer would be dismayed if his crops never yielded their harvest.

Genesis 11:31 tells us that Terah started out with Abraham for the land of Canaan. Verse 31 reads, "And they came unto Haran, and dwelt there." Verse 32 says, "And Terah died in Haran." It sometimes seems that many today are stopping at Haran and dying there. There is no time or place to stop growing. Growth is according to nature's law and God's plan.

How to Grow

1. Naturally

Jesus said, "Consider the lilies of the field, how they grow; they toil not, neither do they spin: and yet I say unto you, That even Solomon in all his glory was not arrayed like one of these" (Matthew 6:28-29).

Notice the phrase "how they grow." Well, how

How to Grow in the Christian Life

do the lilies grow? What is their secret of growth? The lily, according to God's plan, simply unfolds the life within. We do not tell a lily to grow; it grows naturally, spontaneously. It does not fuss or fret, toil or turn, strain or stretch; it just grows. Growth is natural and inevitable when there is life, and more so when there is divine life.

Environment is an important factor in the growing process. If I see an acorn lying on the sidewalk, I know that the acorn will never grow; but put the acorn in the ground where it belongs and it will grow. If we tear a plant out of the soil and hide it from the sun, it will not grow. In just the same way, we who have received Christ must abide in Him if we are to grow and bring forth fruit.

The child of God must continue in a right relationship with God. We are to be rooted in the Word of God. We are to be warmed by the Sun of Righteousness. We are to make friends of God's children. We are to cooperate in every way with the divine Gardener. Do not permit any obstacles to come between you and your Lord. Keep "looking unto Jesus the author and finisher of our faith" (Hebrews 12:2). Then we will bring forth fruit, "some an hundredfold, some sixtyfold, some thirtyfold" (Matthew 13:8).

Salvation is just the beginning of what God wants to do for you. He "is able to do exceeding abundantly above all that we [could] ask or think" (Ephesians 3:20). Before each believer is the limitless ocean of grace and truth. May we never be content with the empty shells on the beach when we can launch out in the deep.

The Bible compares Christians to trees. Our roots are to penetrate the topsoil of truth and stretch down into the great doctrinal rocks of eternal salvation. Then when the hurricane of God's wrath tears up the hypocrites and hurls them into the sea of destruction, those trees planted by God will stand.

As trees we need to throw back our heads and look to Jesus for refreshment. We need to spread our branches out and let the shadow of our holy influence be felt far and near. Our branches should be heavy with fruit. God's promise is, "He shall grow as the lily, and cast forth his roots as Lebanon. His branches shall spread, and his beauty shall be as the olive tree, and his smell as Lebanon. They that dwell under his shadow shall return; they shall revive as the corn, and grow as the vine: the scent thereof shall be as the wine of Lebanon" (Hosea 14:5-7).

2. By eating

We also grow by eating. All living things eat, and what we eat affects our growth. The Bible says, "Eat . . . that which is good" (Isaiah 55:22). There is no book which can make you grow like the Bible.

If we would place the most costly silk under a microscope, it would appear rough and stained. The lily petal under the same lens is flawless. Solomon's royal robes could not compare with God's wild lilies. Matthew 6:28 tells us to "consider the lilies of the field, how they grow." Well, how do they grow? The lily's threadlike roots dig down to the minerals and practice selection. Some minerals look fine, but in reality they are poisonous. They are refused. Others are necessary and they are received. This is exactly what we must do to grow in grace.

There are appealing things that are deadly to growth. The apostle Peter points out some things to refuse: "Laying aside all malice, and all guile, and hypocrisies, and envies, and all evil speakings." Others are to be received: "As newborn babes, desire the sincere milk of the word, that ye may grow thereby" (1 Peter 2:1-2). Whatever else it means, it means that the Word of God is a good thing to feed on. Milk is a food that has been digested by another. Often Christians think that the only feeding they need is that which the pastor has digested and presents on Sunday morning. This is not enough. "Search the scriptures; for in them ye think ye have eternal life: and they are they which testify of me" (John 5:39).

We are to feed on the meat of the Word. D. L. Moody used to hoe potatoes when a boy, and he said that he hoed them so poorly that he always had to mark where he stopped. I wonder, is that how we read the Bible?

3. *By breathing*

What breathing is to the physical man, prayer is to the spiritual man. Our Savior was a man of prayer. The common atmosphere was stifling to Him, and so He frequently sought communion with God in places apart from the crowd. If Jesus, the sinless Son of God, found prayer important, we sinful creatures dare not live without it.

We need to breathe deeply the air from heaven

every day. Andrew Murray said, "We are to be shut out from men, and shut in with God." Archbishop Trench said, "Prayer is not overcoming God's reluctance: it is laying hold of His highest willingness."

Yes, we shall grow if there is communion with Jesus Christ. He is the breath of life. Rubinstein, the great musician, said, "If I omit practice one day, I notice it; if two days, my friends notice it; if three days, the public notices it." This is an old truth, but still vital. We must "pray without ceasing" (1 Thessalonians 5:17). Someone else has said, "Prayer is the preface to the book of Christian living, the text of the new life sermon, the girding on of the armor for battle, the pilgrim's preparation for his journey; and it must be supplemented by action or it amounts to nothing."

Prayer and work form the unbeatable New Testament combination. True prayers never come creeping home.

> Oh, the pure delight of a single hour
> That before Thy throne I spend;
> When I kneel in prayer, and with Thee, my God,
> I commune as friend with friend.
>
> FANNY J. CROSBY

4. By resting

This is what Jesus was talking about when He asked, "Which of you by taking thought can add one cubit unto his stature?" (Matthew 6:27). Anxiety will not add to your spiritual size; worry will not add one fraction to your stature.

The Christian life is not a nervous, hanging-on-to-God, but a resting-in-the-hollow-of-His-hand. I will not grow by toiling and turning, stretching and straining, but rather by yielding completely to Christ's control.

If there is life and health in the physical body, growth is natural and inevitable. So it is spiritually. If we have been born again and are healthy Christians, we will unfold naturally, as the lily from the bud. The Bible says, "Rest in the LORD, and wait patiently for him" (Psalm 37:7). "Underneath are the everlasting arms" (Deuteronomy 33:27). "He giveth his beloved sleep" (Psalm 127:2). "The righteous shall flourish like the palm tree: he shall grow like a cedar in Lebanon. Those that be planted in the house of the LORD shall flourish in the courts of our God. They shall still bring forth in old age; they shall be fat and flourishing" (Psalm 92:12-14).

5. By exercising

The Bible places great stress on work. Show me a person who does not work and I will show you a person who is weak. If you faithfully work, you will eat and sleep right. People often complain that they are not spiritually fed, but probably they are not spiritually hungry, and they are not hungry because they are not working. Broken-down tissues call for nourishment. So those broken down in toil in the Lord's harvest field call out for the bread of life. If a believer will sincerely work in the vineyard of God, he will grow in grace. My friend, if you really want to grow, begin to work. Practice the truth you know, and many other things will become clearer. The farmer's arms become stronger by continual labor. The child grows by exercise. We are to grow as babies grow: slowly and steadily, but surely; a little each day, and a lot in a year. At first the legs may be weak, but soon we will walk without being weary and run without fainting. "He that hath, to him shall be given" (Mark 4:25). Jesus said, "My Father worketh hitherto, and I work" (John 5:17).

One good way to exercise is to *witness* concerning our faith in Jesus Christ. Jesus plainly said, "Ye shall be witnesses unto me" (Acts 1:8). A witness is one who tells what he knows. After everything else is said and done, our real excuse for living is to witness. Do not permit a day to pass without speaking to someone about Jesus Christ. Witnessing keeps the prayer life alive and up to date. It also challenges one to dig into the Scriptures in search of answers for those to whom you are witnessing.

Friend, since your conversion, have you been growing? Are you glorifying God more this week than last week? Are you nearer the Savior now than at your hour of decision? Is your delight in the law of the Lord and are you meditating upon it day and night?

With God's help, Christians can be like trees planted by the rivers of water, spreading forth foliage and bearing fruit. Apart from Christ, we are chaff, without any hope of life.

I would encourage you to grow, grow, grow until that wonderful day when we shall see Him and be like Him!

If God can make of an ugly seed,
With a bit of earth and air

How to Grow in the Christian Life

And dew and rain, sunshine and shade,
A flower so wondrous fair,
What can He make of a soul like you,
With the Bible and faith and prayer,
And the Holy Spirit, if you do His will
And trust in His love and care.

AUTHOR UNKNOWN

REMINDERS

Dead things cannot grow. Before there can be spiritual growth, there must be spiritual life.

We need to grow because growth is *God's plan*. We must bend or be broken.

Salvation is just the beginning of what God wants to do for you.

No book will make you grow like *the Bible*.

"Prayer is not overcoming God's reluctance: it is laying hold of His highest willingness."

ARCHBISHOP TRENCH

Prayer and work is the unbeatable New Testament combination. True prayers never come creeping home.

QUESTIONS

1. What is the very first necessary step for growth?
2. Give three verses that show that God intends Christians to grow.
3. Why is a study of the Bible compared to food?

The Basics of the Christian Life

4. Illustrate from the life of Jesus the importance of prayer. *like breathing*
5. What effect can witnessing have on our prayer and Bible study? *deepen it*
6. List five suggestions for growth.
7. How does God want us to grow, according to 2 Peter 3:18?
8. What are the things that prevent growth in nature? In spirit? *food/water — Word/Light*
9. What does it mean to "rest in the Lord" (Psalm 37:7)? How can we both rest and work?
10. In what ways can we exercise our faith?

6. naturally — environment
eating — Word
reading — Prayer
resting — meditate / let it go
exercising — witnessing

4

You and the Holy Spirit

In whom ye also are builded together for an habitation of God through the Spirit.

EPHESIANS 2:22

When Dwight L. Moody was visiting England, he heard Henry Varley say: "The world has yet to see what God will do with a man who is fully and wholly consecrated to the Holy Spirit."

Moody would later comment, "He said 'a man.' He did not say 'a great man,' nor 'a learned man,' nor a 'rich man,' but simply 'a man.' I am a man, and it lies within the man himself whether he will or will not make that entire and full consecration. I will try my utmost to be that man."

* * *

Every Christian must rely upon the Holy Spirit because He is indispensable. He is the chief Architect in building a life. And yet, for many people, the Holy Spirit is the forgotten member of the Trinity. His ministry is either unknown or ignored, and therefore His power unused.

In the preface to his paraphrase of the New Testament epistles, J. B. Phillips writes,

> The great difference between present-day Christianity and that of which we read in these letters is that to us it is primarily a performance, to them it was a real experience. . . . To these men it is quite plainly the invasion of their lives by a new quality of life altogether. They do not hesitate to describe this as Christ "living in" them.[1]

What a rebuke to us. As I read this I could not help but ask myself, "What kind of Christian am I? Am I experiencing the all-powerful presence of God through the Holy Spirit?"

Down through the centuries there have been many examples of Christians who, although their lives were quite ordinary, were transformed by the power of the Holy Spirit into vibrant believers—active and energetic witnesses for Jesus Christ.

Take Peter, for example. Before the Holy Spirit took charge of him at Pentecost, he had been a disciple. But he had also denied Jesus. He had been ashamed to stand for Jesus Christ.

But when the Holy Spirit got hold of Peter, he became a different man. A fantastic change came over him, and he began to powerfully preach the gospel of Jesus Christ.

Some time ago I received a letter from a young man. "For twenty of my thirty-three years," he said, "I have been a professing Christian. But not until recently did I really understand the work of the Holy Spirit or what He could do in my life. The

---

1. J. B. Phillips, *Letters to Young Churches* (New York: Macmillan, 1950), p. xiv.

difference He has made in my life has been unbelievable."

Each believer must realize that the Holy Spirit dwells within, and that He is willing and waiting to be our Helper and Guide. Conversion to Jesus Christ began in us with the regenerating power of the Holy Spirit, and it continues and will conclude by His resurrection power.

THE HOLY SPIRIT IN THE OLD TESTAMENT

During Old Testament times the Spirit of God was active, but apparently in a limited way. For example, He was present in creation, for Scripture says, "And the Spirit of God moved upon the face of the waters" (Genesis 1:2). Of Samson we read, "And the Spirit of the LORD came mightily upon him" (Judges 14:6). Then, too, certain men were said to possess the Spirit of God. For instance, Joshua: "And the LORD said unto Moses, Take thee Joshua the son of Nun, a man in whom is the spirit, and lay thine hand upon him" (Numbers 27:18). The Old Testament contains at least eighty-eight references to the Holy Spirit. These references seem to show that the Holy Spirit would come for a specific task and then leave when the work was complete. In the New Testament the relationship to the Spirit is constant and abiding.

The Spirit of God was the Spirit of conviction while sin worked itself out from Fall to Flood; He was a Spirit of detailed service while the people of God were being organized into a nationality; He was a Spirit of strength while the people were fighting for the land, and were casting out those who had deeply sinned; and He became a Spirit of hope when the peculiar people had passed into a condition of apostasy and wandering. He lit the horizon with the glow of approaching day.[2]

THE HOLY SPIRIT AS PROMISED BY JESUS

There is no doubt that the Spirit of God was active in the Old Testament; however, Jesus promised that the Holy Spirit would come in a different way than ever before. In fact, Jesus said that it was expedient, or better, for His disciples that He go away, for if He did not go away, the Spirit would not come (John 16:7).

John the apostle verified this when he said the Holy Spirit was not yet given "because that Jesus was not yet glorified" (John 7:39). This passage makes it clear that the Holy Spirit was to come and be active in a different way than ever before. The fulfillment of this promise took place at Pentecost.

In the first chapter of the book of Acts, the disciples were commanded to wait for the coming of the Holy Spirit. The second chapter tells the thrilling story of His arrival (Acts 2:1-4).

From that day to this the Holy Spirit has *never* departed. He has been with the church ever since. Often He is grieved because of unbelief, but He is *never* absent. Pentecost marked the coming of the Spirit in a new way to live in the earthly bodies of all believers. Joyfully we can sing:

---

2. G. Campbell Morgan, *The Spirit of God* (New York: Revell, 1900), p. 93.

> O spread the tidings 'round,
> wherever man is found,
> Wherever human hearts
> and human woes abound;
> Let every Christian tongue
> proclaim the joyful sound:
> The Comforter has come!
>
> — FRANK BOTTOME

THE HOLY SPIRIT IS A PERSON

The Holy Spirit possesses all the characteristics of personality. He has intellect and will. He possesses emotion. He is not some vague force. He is not an impersonal power or energy like electricity or gravity.

The Holy Spirit is also our *Teacher*. "But the Comforter, which is the Holy Ghost, whom the Father will send in my name, he shall . . . bring all things to your remembrance, whatsoever I have said unto you" (John 14:26).

The Holy Spirit assures us of personal salvation. In Romans 8:16, we read, "The Spirit itself beareth witness with our spirit, that we are the children of God." The Holy Spirit agrees with our spirit if we are in tune with God.

Again in John 16, Jesus taught that the Holy Spirit convinces men of sin. When the Holy Spirit comes, said Jesus, "He will reprove the world of sin, and of righteousness, and of judgment" (v. 8).

The Holy Spirit teaches us, strengthens us, witnesses within us. Yes, the Holy Spirit has particular characteristics and functions. The Bible clearly teaches that *He is a person*.

THE HOLY SPIRIT INDWELLS ALL BELIEVERS

The Bible plainly teaches that each believer is the dwelling place of the Holy Spirit. What a staggering truth! Think of it—God the Holy Spirit indwelling every Christian!

To the carnal Corinthians, Paul wrote, "Know ye not that ye are the temple of God, and that the Spirit of God dwelleth in you?" (1 Corinthians 3:16). In spite of their carnality, they were still the dwelling place of the Holy Spirit.

In past history God dwelt in the Tabernacle and then later on in the Temple. You may ask, "Where does He dwell now?" The Bible says, "in you." "Christ in you, the hope of glory" (Colossians 1:27). Whether you are eight years of age or eighty, the moment you receive Christ, the Holy Spirit takes up His dwelling in your earthly body.

The word *dwell* is a beautiful word. It means to settle down and live, as you would at home. The Holy Spirit is a personal, permanent Guest. He is with us and in us *all the time*.

As a living Resident within the believer, the Holy Spirit gives strength for our weaknesses. He guides us in understanding God's Word and God's will. He helps us to pray. He empowers us to serve. He comforts us in our sorrow. He is the Paraclete, the One sent to assist us in every area of our lives.

More happened when you received Christ than you ever realized. First, you received the forgiveness of sins. Second, you instantly became a member of the great family of God. Third, you were sealed with the Holy Spirit. Paul said, "In whom also after that ye believed, ye were sealed with that

You and the Holy Spirit

holy Spirit of promise" (Ephesians 1:13). This speaks of divine ownership.

Paul continues, "The temple of God is holy, which temple ye are" (1 Corinthians 3:17). Paul is simply telling us that our lives must be holy. Always remember, He is the Holy Spirit, and He requires cleanness of life. The Bible says, "Walk in the Spirit, and ye shall not fulfil the lust of the flesh" (Galatians 5:16).

THE HOLY SPIRIT AND THE STRUGGLE AHEAD

There is within every Christian a *conflict!* The apostle Paul gives us a picture of this in Romans 7. Although the believer has been completely forgiven, he soon discovers that sin is still active within him. Although we are changed because of conversion, we are not all that we shall be someday. Sin continues to work in us, and the result is a battle between the "new nature" with all its new ideals and aspirations and the "old nature" with its desires and expectations.

The Christian wants to please God, whereas the unconverted man seeks to please himself.

Is there a way out? Are we destined to be victims of our sinful natures, or can we be victors? What a thrill it is to know that *victory is absolutely possible!* It is available to all.

First, to be victorious you must submit your life to Jesus Christ and receive Him as Savior. Someone has said, "If you would master temptation, you must first let Christ master you."

Mankind is like a clock whose mainspring is

broken. He needs to be totally renewed on the inside, but the repairs must be supplied from without. He cannot save himself. Even so, men and women today need someone to remake them. That someone is Jesus Christ, the Redeemer of man's soul and nature. He loves you, He died for you, and He wants you to turn to Him in repentance and faith.

Salvation is the first step to victory over temptation.

Second, to the believer—the child of God—is given the privilege of prayer in overcoming temptation. James says, "If any of you lack wisdom, let him *ask of God*, that giveth to all men liberally" (James 1:5).

Do you need help in overcoming your weakness? *Ask God!* Do you need deliverance from the power and temptation of sin? Ask God! He alone is able to deliver you. Often I have cried out, "Lord help me," and God's deliverance was given.

God's Word proclaims that "there hath no temptation taken you but such as is common to man: but God is faithful, who will not suffer you to be tempted above that ye are able; but will with the temptation also make a way of escape, that ye may be able to bear it" (1 Corinthians 10:13).

D. L. Moody once said, "When Christians find themselves exposed to temptation they should pray to God to uphold them, and when they are tempted they should not be discouraged. It is not a sin to be tempted; the sin is to fall into temptation."

Third, apply the Word of God. Jesus put Satan to

flight by quoting Scripture. Jesus said, "It is written," and so must we fortify ourselves with the Word of God.

Fourth, submit to the indwelling Holy Spirit. When a drop of water falls on a hot stove, the water never really touches the stove. It rests on a thin cushion of very hot air. Heat overcomes gravity and holds the water away until it evaporates. To the child of God who is directed by the Holy Spirit, temptation may come but it will not be able to destroy us. For God has promised, "Greater is he that is in you, than he that is in the world" (1 John 4:4).

In your hour of trial, remember that God is faithful. He knows your capacity. He will give you all the strength you need to overcome temptation, or He will make a way of deliverance for you.

The secret of victory in your Christian life is in the *indwelling Holy Spirit*. Allow Him to have undisputed control of your whole life.

THE HOLY SPIRIT EMPOWERS FOR SERVICE

A. C. Dixon used to say, "When we rely on organization, we get what organization can do. When we rely on eloquence, we get what eloquence can do. But when we rely on the Holy Spirit, we get *what God can do.*"

Power is within reach of all who believe. Our departing Lord said, "Ye shall receive power, after that the Holy Ghost is come upon you" (Acts 1:8).

I heard a true story not long ago of a man who for several years had struggled to keep his rather large lawn mowed. Finally he decided it just wasn't worth all the time and trouble. He determined that he was going to buy one of those nice riding lawn mowers, something that would take all the headache out of his Saturday afternoons.

Well, he did just that. And the day came for the delivery of his new machine. The man who brought it told him just how it should be operated, explaining all the controls and also pointing out that it was already filled with gas and oil.

Well, the man could hardly wait to try out his new mower. As soon as the delivery man left, he jumped into the seat and turned the key, but nothing happened. No engine started, no noise, nothing!

His first reaction was to check the gas and oil. They were fine. Then he examined the key and turned it back and forth. Still nothing! Finally he decided that despite the fact that the mower was brand new, the battery must be dead. So he took the battery to the nearest service station and had it charged, came home, turned the key—and again nothing happened.

As he was just about to reach his wit's end, his neighbor came over and asked him what his trouble was. After explaining all he had been through, the neighbor climbed onto the mower, turned the key, pushed the starter, and immediately the engine began to purr.

The owner was completely flabbergasted! To think, all that trouble simply because he failed to push the starter button.

"How simple," you say, and you are absolutely right! But, what the starter button was to that lawn mower, the Holy Spirit is in the life of the believer! Just as the machine needed the contact of power to operate, so we need the power of the Holy Spirit to serve successfully in the Christian life.

As we depend on the Holy Spirit we shall be empowered to live above the world, the flesh, and the devil. In our strength we will surely fall, but "if ye through the Spirit do mortify the deeds of the body, ye shall live" (Romans 8:13). The Holy Spirit is our source of power.

A Word of Warning

We must always remember that the Holy Spirit may be grieved because of careless living. Paul warns, "And grieve not the holy Spirit of God, whereby ye are sealed unto the day of redemption" (Ephesians 4:30). The word *grieve* means to "cause sorrow." G. Campbell Morgan asks, "How would you like to be compelled to live with somebody who was everlastingly grieving your heart by his conduct?" Do not grieve or quench the indwelling Holy Spirit; rather, "be filled with the Spirit" (Ephesians 5:18).

The blessed Holy Spirit is our Helper *today, tomorrow,* and *always.* Open wide every area of your life, and He will fill it with His presence.

Reminders

"The world has yet to see what God will do with a man who is fully and wholly consecrated to the Holy Spirit."

Henry Varley

> Pentecost marked the coming of the Spirit in a new way to live in the earthly bodies of all believers.
>
> "When we rely on organization, we get what organization can do. When we rely upon education, we get what education can do. When we rely on eloquence, we get what eloquence can do. But when we rely on the Holy Spirit, we get what God can do."
>
> A. C. Dixon
>
> The secret of victory in your Christian life is the indwelling Holy Spirit, permitting Him to have undisputed control of your whole life.
>
> Though we are not sinless, we should sin less and less.

Questions

1. Describe in your own words the difference between the work of the Holy Spirit before and after Pentecost.
2. Why was it better for Jesus to ascend to heaven?
3. How would you show that the Holy Spirit is a person?
4. When does the Holy Spirit indwell a believer and for how long?
5. Why do believers in Christ still experience inner conflicts?
6. List a few things the Holy Spirit does for us.
7. What does it mean to be "sealed" with the Holy Spirit (Ephesians 1:13)?

8. If we have the Holy Spirit within us, why do we still have internal conflicts?
9. How do we get the power that the Holy Spirit has to offer?
10. What does it mean to "grieve" the Holy Spirit (Ephesians 4:30)? How can we prevent this?

5
You and Your Bible

Whosoever heareth these sayings of mine, and doeth them, I will liken him unto a wise man, which built his house upon a rock.

MATTHEW 7:24

Luther studied the Bible as one would gather apples: "First I shake the whole tree, that the ripest might fall. Then I climb the tree and shake each limb, and then each branch and then each twig, and then I look under each leaf."

* * *

The Bible is literally *God speaking to you*. It is God's instrument in salvation (Romans 10:17; 1 Peter 1:25) and God's instrument for growing mature Christians (1 Peter 2:2). It is the blueprint for the Christian.

The very first step in understanding the Bible is *conversion*. Paul said, "But the natural man receiveth not the things of the Spirit of God: for they are foolishness unto him: neither can he know them, because they are spiritually discerned. But he that is spiritual judgeth all things" (1 Corinthians 2:14-15).

The unsaved person can read the Bible and receive considerable inspiration, but the true Christian receives infinitely more. To salvation must be added *submission*. The Bible must be read in a spirit of humility. This is the way to begin:

READ THE BIBLE PRAYERFULLY

Prayer is the "open sesame" to the Bible. *Always* begin your Bible reading with prayer for divine guidance. All of us in reading some current book have wished the author were present to answer and explain some things, but this is rarely possible. Amazing as it seems, this *is possible* when reading the Bible. James said, "If any of you lack wisdom, let him ask of God, that giveth to all men liberally, and upbraideth not; and it shall be given him" (James 1:5). God really wants to give us wisdom and understanding. The psalmist knew this truth, for long years ago he prayed, "Open thou mine eyes, that I may behold wondrous things out of thy law" (Psalm 119:18). It is really wonderful to ask the Lord to show us some "wondrous thing" each day out of His law. After God does this for us, think about this truth, apply it, and put it to use.

* * *

John Newton said it this way: "By one hour's intimate access to the throne of grace, where the Lord causes His glory to pass before the soul that seeks Him, you may acquire more true spiritual knowledge and comfort than by a day's or a week's converse with the best of men, or the most studious perusal of many folios."

* * *

The Bible is the result of men being moved by the Holy Spirit. In 2 Peter 1:21 we read, "For the prophecy came not in old time by the will of man: but the holy men of God spake as they were moved by the Holy Ghost." And again, "All scripture is given by inspiration of God" (2 Timothy 3:16). The very same Holy Spirit who led those men to write, longs to lead us *today* so we can understand. Without the Holy Spirit, the Bible is like an ocean which cannot be sounded, heavens which cannot be surveyed, mines which cannot be explored, and mysteries beyond unraveling. We must—we must—yield to the leadership of the Holy Spirit. Jesus said, "When he, the Spirit of truth, is come, he will guide you into all truth" (John 16:13). The Holy Spirit has come and dwells in every believer. Permit Him to guide you into God's truth. Without the illumination of the Holy Spirit, we read in vain. So read the Bible prayerfully.

Read the Bible Carefully

Of the Christians at Berea it could be said, "These were more noble than those in Thessalonica, in that they received the word with all readiness of mind, and searched the scriptures daily, whether those things were so" (Acts 17:11). The

Bereans read the Scriptures carefully! Today the Bible is read a lot but studied little. To read with care requires concentration, so our minds must be alert. To read in a perfunctory way for the sake of conscience is not worth much.

Jesus said, "If any man will do his will, he shall know of the doctrine, whether it be of God, or whether I speak of myself" (John 7:17). This requires obedience. "If any man will do his will, he shall know." All the icebergs of difficulty will melt before a ready and willing mind. Dark skies will be pierced, deep places fathomed, and wide rivers forded. Obedience to God's will results in an unshakable confidence in God's Word.

The Bereans also "searched the scriptures daily." This requires work, for the great truths of God are not discovered by the casual reader. Diamonds are not found on the sidewalk. The best is always under the shell. We must linger upon the Bible's chapters, verses, phrases, and words, eagerly seeking to understand its message. Yes, we must search like a miner looking for gold. The psalmist said, "I love thy commandments above gold" (Psalm 119:127). We must search like a hungry man does for food. Jeremiah said, "Thy words were found, and I did eat them" (Jeremiah 15:16). Job said, "I have esteemed the words of his mouth more than my necessary food" (Job 23:12). And again, "How sweet are thy words unto my taste! Yea, sweeter than honey to my mouth!" (Psalm 119:103). The little bee alights on the flower, then dips down to the very heart and sucks up the honey. Careful Bible reading will yield honey to the mouth. Jesus said, "Search the scriptures; for in them ye think ye have eternal life" (John 5:39).

The Lord's formula for Joshua's success was: "This book of the law shall not depart out of thy mouth; but thou shalt meditate therein day and night, that thou mayest observe to do according to all that is written therein: for then thou shalt make thy way prosperous, and then thou shalt have good success" (Joshua 1:8).

The word *meditate* means "to attend." All attention must be focused on the subject at hand. David's definition of a happy man in Psalm 1 is one whose "delight is in the law of the Lord; and in his law doth he meditate day and night." May God deliver us from a complacent, casual, cursory reading of the Word of God. Let us read the Bible carefully.

READ THE BIBLE SYSTEMATICALLY

First, let me suggest that you set aside a definite time for Bible reading, preferably at the beginning of the day when the mind is alert. At a prescribed time, in a quiet place, systematically read the Word of God.

Do not permit anything to interfere, no matter how important it seems. Many well-meaning Christians who sincerely love the Lord are up and down in their Christian experience because they have no definite time with God. The old hymn states, "Take time to be holy, Speak oft with thy Lord." To this we could add, make time. Let us beware of the barrenness of an overactive life.

To read a portion of the Bible before retiring is fine but not sufficient. Not only should our last conscious thoughts be of the Lord, but also our first thoughts. Give God the first part of the day, not the last; the best, not the worst. "But they that wait upon the LORD shall renew their strength; they shall mount up with wings as eagles; they shall run, and not be weary; and they shall walk, and not faint" (Isaiah 40:31).

Second, begin at the beginning. In reading any other book we start with chapter 1. To start a novel or biography in the middle results in confusion. The same holds true for the Bible. We cannot adequately understand Exodus apart from Genesis, or Hebrews apart from Leviticus. Too often we become so attached to certain favorite portions that we neglect the remainder of the Bible. Begin where God began, Genesis, chapter 1, verse 1; and steadily go through to Revelation, chapter 22, verse 21.

Third, secure a notebook and jot down some questions such as: Who is speaking: God, an apostle, or the devil? To whom was it written: saints or sinners? What was the background of the writer and possibly the receiver? What are the main ideas? What seems to be the key verse? What message is there for me today? As you read, fill in the answers. Learn the facts; then apply them. This method of reading will help you grasp the entire book, thus avoiding error and misinterpretation. As you read, make sure you understand the words. If not, look them up. Get your bearings geographically and chronologically. Notice the marginal references and compare Scripture with Scripture. Added to your regular reading you might want to do some topical studying. This yields rich dividends. Take your concordance and look up the word *heaven*. Look up every passage in the Bible on this subject and record your findings. You will be thrilled at what you have learned.

Commentaries are splendid; however, beware of being chained to them. Someone has humorously said, "The Bible throws a lot of light on the commentaries." Any book that takes priority over the Bible becomes a crutch which leads to weakness. To read the words of men and neglect the Word of God is to say the books of men are of greater worth. Read the Bible systematically.

READ THE BIBLE TRUSTFULLY

Why? Because "without faith"—WITHOUT FAITH—"it is impossible to please [God]" (Hebrews 11:6). Salvation, as well as Christian growth, depends upon believing. Faith is necessary in understanding the Bible. This is exactly where Israel failed. "The word preached did not profit them, not being mixed with faith in them that heard it" (Hebrews 4:2). We must—we must—believe God! We must read the Bible *trustfully*.

The Bible is living, not dead. If the Lord came personally to you, would you ignore Him? Well, God has spoken to you in the Bible! May we never neglect it. Just think of it! Not man's word, but God's Word. May we sincerely say with Samuel,

"Speak, LORD; for thy servant heareth" (1 Samuel 3:9).

Just imagine Mr. Jones at the close of a busy day. He is weary in body and fatigued in mind. Just before going to bed he hurriedly reads one of the shorter psalms. Briefly he prays and falls into bed. Doubtless Mr. Jones will remember little of his reading. Every condition militates against it.

In contrast, picture Mr. Jones at the beginning of the day. He is rested in body and ready in mind. In a definite place at a definite time he starts the day with God. After prayer for the Spirit's guidance, he reads with care, answering obvious questions and making brief notations of his findings. Occasionally a verse must be looked up or a passage of Scripture compared with another. After systematic study he is ready for all the events of the day. The Word of God will garrison him against evil. His new spiritual discoveries may be applied and put to use. We can be reasonably sure he will "grow in grace, and in the knowledge of our Lord and Saviour Jesus Christ" (2 Peter 3:18).

To grow in the things of God we should read the Bible *prayerfully, carefully, systematically,* and most of all, *trustfully.*

REMINDERS

The very first step in understanding the Bible is *conversion*.

"By one hour's intimate access to the throne of

> grace, where the Lord causes His glory to pass before the soul that seeks Him, you may acquire more true spiritual knowledge and comfort than by a day's or a week's converse with the best of men, or the most studious perusal of many folios."
>
> JOHN NEWTON
>
> The same Holy Spirit who led these men to write, longs to lead us to *understand*.
>
> The Bereans "searched the scriptures daily" (Acts 17:11). This requires work, for the great truths of God are not discovered by the casual reader. Diamonds are not found on the sidewalk.

QUESTIONS

1. List two verses of Scripture which indicate that the Bible is God's instrument in salvation and Christian growth.
2. Why is conversion the first step in understanding the Bible?
3. In what way is prayer related to an understanding of Scripture (Psalm 119:18)?
4. In what way were the Christians at Berea examples to us today (Acts 17:11)?
5. List three ways in which a Christian should read his Bible.
6. Why is it vital to read the Bible trustfully?

6
How to Pray

Ask, and it shall be given you; seek, and ye shall find; knock, and it shall be opened unto you.
                                              MATTHEW 7:7

Pray for great things, expect great things, work for great things, but above all, pray.
                                              R. A. TORREY

Prayer is the key that unlocks the door to God's treasures.

* * *

The disciples came to Jesus one day and asked, "Lord, teach us to pray" (Luke 11:1). They had noticed that no one ever prayed like Jesus, and as they watched and listened to the prayer of Jesus, they realized their own desperate need. They did not ask, "Lord, teach us to preach," but "Teach us to pray."

At first, prayer may be awkward. The words may come slowly, but keep on praying, for through prayer we can enter into the very presence of God.

We can make our needs known to Him, but, greater still, we can commune with God.

What Is Prayer?

The dictionary describes prayer as a reverent or devout petition to God, an entreaty. Certainly prayer is that. The simplest definition of prayer is the word *cry*. In Romans 8:15, Paul says, "For ye have not received the spirit of bondage again to fear; but ye have received the Spirit of adoption, whereby we *cry*, Abba, Father."

Prayer is a *cry*. When we pray, we are crying out to God. "Lord, help me." "Lord, give me wisdom." "Lord, help me to be silent." Prayer is a cry. Just as a little child cries to his parent, we cry to God.

But prayer is also a *call*. In Jeremiah 33:3, Jehovah's words are: "Call unto me, and I will answer thee, and shew thee great and mighty things, which thou knowest not."

Prayer is *asking*. Again, our Lord said in Luke 11:9, "Ask, and it shall be given you; seek, and ye shall find; knock, and it shall be opened unto you."

But prayer is also *communion*. "How rare it is," said Fenelon, "to find a soul quiet enough to hear God speak." Prayer is talking to God and having Him talk to us. It is spending time in communion with our heavenly Father.

One day the five-year-old son of D. L. Moody went into the study where his father sat writing. Wanting no interruptions, Mr. Moody gruffly asked, "Well, what do you want?"

"Nothing, Daddy," the boy replied. "I just wanted

to be where you are." Sitting on the floor, he began to amuse himself quietly. He desired only companionship.

G. Campbell Morgan, the great English preacher, relates that it was "this little incident, told by Mr. Moody, that helped me greatly to understand the true meaning of prayer. To pray is to be where Jesus is. When we are in His presence, we need nothing more to pray prevailingly."

WHY SHOULD WE PRAY?

The answer to why we should pray is very simple: the Bible teaches us to pray. In Luke 18:1, Jesus said, "Men ought always to pray, and not to faint." Prayer is God's cure for caving in. In Matthew 9:38 we are admonished to pray that the Lord of the harvest will send forth laborers into His harvest.

Why pray? The answer is, because Jesus prayed. His entire life on earth was an example of prayer.

Since Jesus Christ, the sinless Son of God, found prayer important, we sinful creatures find prayer indispensable! Jesus prayed at the beginning of His public ministry when He was baptized: "Now when all the people were baptized, it came to pass, that Jesus also being baptized, and praying, the heaven was opened" (Luke 3:21).

Before choosing the twelve apostles, He spent all night in prayer: "And it came to pass in those days, that he went out into a mountain to pray, and continued all night in prayer to God. And when it was day, he called unto him his disciples: and of them he chose twelve, whom also he named apostles" (Luke 6:12-13).

He prayed before feeding the 5,000: "And Jesus took the loaves; and when he had given thanks, he distributed to the disciples, and the disciples to them that were set down; and likewise of the fishes as much as they would" (John 6:11). Jesus prayed before rescuing the disciples at sea. The Bible says, "He went up into a mountain apart to pray" (Matthew 14:23).

At the grave of Lazarus, He prayed: "Then they took away the stone from the place where the dead was laid. And Jesus lifted up his eyes, and said, Father, I thank thee that thou hast heard me" (John 11:41).

At the Last Supper, Jesus prayed: "And as they did eat, Jesus took bread, and blessed, and brake it, and gave to them, and said, Take, eat: this is my body" (Mark 14:22).

In Gethsemane, Jesus agonized in prayer (Matthew 26:36-44). Our Lord prayed often, and so must each Christian learn to pray.

Why pray? Because even now, Jesus Christ is praying for us, *right now*. The Bible says, "He ever liveth to make intercession for them" (Hebrews 7:25).

Why pray? Because prayer was the example given to us by *the early church*. Of the apostolic Church we read, "And they continued stedfastly in the apostles' doctrine and fellowship, and in breaking of bread, and in prayers" (Acts 2:42). Before the day of Pentecost they gathered together to pray: "These all continued with one accord in prayer and supplication, with the women, and Mary the mother of Jesus, and with his brethren" (Acts 1:14).

After Pentecost they "continued stedfastly" in prayer.

When Peter was jailed, they prayed until God delivered him: "And when he had considered the thing, he came to the house of Mary the mother of John, whose surname was Mark; where many were gathered together praying" (Acts 12:12).

The apostolic church saturated their efforts with prayer. The apostle James told the Christians of his time that their spiritual poverty was due to neglect of prayer. "Ye have not, because ye ask not" (James 4:2).

How Should We Pray?

1. We should pray humbly.

The apostle James tells us that "God resisteth the proud, but giveth grace unto the humble" (4:6). Have you ever had anyone resist you? At every opportunity he fought you; he was totally disagreeable. That is a very difficult situation to be in. But there is nothing—absolutely nothing—so hopeless as having God resist you.

God's prescription for spiritual blessing is outlined in 2 Chronicles 7:14: "If my people, which are called by my name, shall humble themselves, and pray."

The first key to fruitful praying is a spirit of humility.

2. We should pray specifically.

Robert Cook tells of a missionary who was evacuated during World War II from a South Pacific island. He was put on a freighter that zigzagged through enemy waters in its journey to safety. One day, right before the ship, there appeared the periscope of an enemy submarine.

"That's when I learned to pray specifically," said the missionary. "While the enemy was looking our ship over (probably trying to decide whether or not to sink us) we prayed over every inch of that sub. 'Lord, stop his motors!' 'Jam his torpedo tubes!' 'Break his rudder!' "

That missionary prayed specifically. Why? Because he had a specific need—his life was in danger.

Our prayers don't need to be long. Many of our Lord's prayers were only a few words. The important thing is that they be *specific*.

3. We should pray believingly.

General Booth, founder of the Salvation Army, advised people to "work as if everything depended upon your work, and pray as if everything depended upon your prayer."

Pray—expecting God to answer!

In Hebrews 11:6 we are told that "without faith it is impossible to please him: for he that cometh to God must believe that he is, and that he is a rewarder of them that diligently seek him."

James says, "But let him ask in faith, nothing wavering. For he that wavereth is like a wave of the sea driven with the wind and tossed. For let not that man think that he shall receive any thing of the Lord" (James 1:6-7).

It was said of Praying Hyde, missionary to India, "He prayed as if God were at his elbow," standing ready to answer. He had faith!

Without faith—we cannot be saved.
Without faith—we cannot grow.
Without faith—we cannot please God.
Without faith—we will have no answer to our prayers.
Pray *believingly!*

4. *We should pray intelligently.*

When we pray we should determine, "What do I really want from God?" When I consult my doctor or lawyer, I carefully prepare my questions so that all my needs will be met. When we talk to God we should intelligently bring our requests and petitions before Him. Again James says, "Ye ask, and receive not, because ye ask amiss" (James 4:3). Which brings me to another important point. We need to ask ourselves, "Can God grant my request?" For example, you should not pray, "Lord, make my husband become a Christian." God doesn't work that way. You ought rather to pray, "Lord, help me to lovingly relate the gospel to my husband so he might accept You as his Savior."

We also need to ask, "Have I done my part? Am I setting the proper example? Am I demonstrating Christ's love in my life?"

If a man prays for God to give him a job, he must be willing to read the want ads. The Lord always expects us to do our part in prayer.

5. *We should pray obediently.*

There is no way we can be successful in our prayer life if we are living with unconfessed sin.

The psalmist declared, "If I regard iniquity in my heart, the Lord will not hear me" (Psalm 66:18). Sin—unconfessed sin—is disobedience. Sin blocks our communication with God. It knocks down the power lines.

Jesus said, "If ye love me, keep my commandments" (John 14:15). We need to pray to God from an obedient heart.

When Should We Pray?

It would be difficult to pray in the wrong place or at the wrong time. Jonah prayed powerfully in the belly of the fish. Paul and Silas prayed at midnight in the dungeon.

We can pray anytime, anywhere. However, it is best to have a definite time and place for daily prayer. David said, "Evening, and morning, and at noon, will I pray, and cry aloud: and he shall hear my voice" (Psalm 55:17).

Of Daniel we read, "Now when Daniel knew that the writing was signed, he went into his house; and his windows being open in his chamber toward Jerusalem, he kneeled upon his knees three times a day, and prayed, and gave thanks before his God, as he did aforetime" (Daniel 6:10).

Jesus has told us to enter into the private place to pray. "But thou, when thou prayest, enter into thy closet, and when thou hast shut thy door, pray to thy Father which is in secret; and thy Father which seeth in secret shall reward thee openly" (Matthew 6:6).

Whenever God's people gather, whether to eat,

to study the Bible, or to socialize, it is right to pray, asking God's blessing.

Do not forget the need for family prayer, a practice which draws the family together with a common cord.

For What Shall We Pray?

We are to pray for all things needful for our physical and spiritual welfare. "If ye then, being evil, know how to give good gifts unto your children, how much more shall your Father which is in heaven give good things to them that ask him?" (Matthew 7:11).

Jesus taught His disciples to pray for their daily bread. This infers the needs of life: food, clothing, and shelter. Nothing is too large or too small for God. We are invited to take everything to God in prayer.

Obstacles to Prayer

Prayer is not easy; it is difficult. Unbelief, worldliness, and indifference render prayer useless.

Consider the following Bible verses: "Behold, the Lord's hand is not shortened, that it cannot save; neither his ear heavy, that it cannot hear: but your iniquities have separated between you and your God, and your sins have hid his face from you, that he will not hear" (Isaiah 59:1-2). "If I regard iniquity in my heart, the Lord will not hear me" (Psalm 66:18). "For the eyes of the Lord are over the righteous, and his ears are open unto their prayers: but the face of the Lord is against them that do evil" (1 Peter 3:12).

Sin causes mankind to be lost, and sin in the believer's life makes prayer worthless. Thus it forms a vicious cycle. Ask God to keep you from sin.

Prayer is a gracious privilege. It is a glorious calling. *Cultivate prayer.*

REMINDERS

Prayer is the key that unlocks the door to God's treasures.

The simplest definition of prayer is the three-letter word *cry*.

"Work as if everything depended upon your work and pray as if everything depended upon your prayer."

GENERAL WILLIAM BOOTH

The first key to fruitful praying is a spirit of *humility*.

Sin blocks our communication with God. It knocks down the power lines.

Prayer is not only our privilege, but it is our duty. Neglect of prayer is disobedience which displeases God.

QUESTIONS

1. Give two biblical definitions of prayer as found in Romans 8:15 and Jeremiah 33:3.

How to Pray

2. List at least three reasons why we should pray and verify these with Scripture.
3. Share five areas of concern under the heading "How Should I Pray?"
4. According to James 1:6-17, what is a key element in prayer?
5. What are some general areas of prayer?
6. Why should we pray specifically?
7. What does it mean to pray intelligently?
8. When is the best time to pray?
9. How do we know what to pray for?
10. List some obstacles to prayer and the solutions.

7
How to Have a Quiet Time

And in the morning, rising up a great while before day, he went out, and departed into a solitary place, and there prayed.

MARK 1:35

Andrew Bonar, a great man of God, had three rules that he lived by. Rule 1—Not to speak to any person before speaking to Jesus Christ. Rule 2- Not to do anything with his hands until he had been on his knees. Rule 3—Not to read the papers until he had read his Bible.

* * *

We live in a fast moving, noisy world!

The pace at which most of us operate is frightening. More than ever before, we need to budget our time to do those things that must be done. Because of our hectic schedules, many important activities often get lost in the shuffle. They're left undone.

Each of us must decide what our priorities will be. We alone determine what will come first in our

How to Have a Quiet Time

lives. Whether to spend time talking with God or to spend time doing something else is a decision each of us must make. We must decide what is primary and what is secondary.

Unfortunately, for many Christians, the quiet time does not rank high enough on the list. It becomes a casualty to the clock. It is often left out of our day. The activity which should be most important to us is put aside, leaving us spiritually weak and sick.

What Is "The Quiet Time"?

The Christian's quiet time is the time he spends sharing with God the Father. It is, more specifically, the definite time set aside each day for prayer, meditation, and the study of God's Word. It is from the quiet time with God that we derive strength, wisdom, and guidance for each day. Without a daily devotional life we become spiritually anemic, starved, and easy prey to the devil.

The quiet time is much like a spiritual shower or bath. It washes, refreshes, and revives us. It helps to protect us from the moral corruption around us. And it prepares us, as Christian soldiers, to engage in a spiritual war.

Yes, my friend, the daily devotional life of the believer is an indispensable ingredient for a successful Christian life. Jesus said, "Man shall not live by bread alone, but by every word that proceedeth out of the mouth of God" (Matthew 4:4).

D. L. Moody once said, "If I can get a man to think for five minutes about his soul, he is almost certain to be converted." Many people have never given their lives to Christ, not because they've never heard the gospel, but because they have never been quiet long enough to consider their need and to let the gospel sink in.

The Christian knows Jesus Christ as his Savior; but unless he spends regular periods in quietness and meditation in the Word of God, he will never know Jesus better.

Louise Smith writes of a woman who had been a Christian for many years. And yet, because of tension and emptiness in her life, she was on the verge of a nervous collapse. As she prayed to the Lord for help, the Holy Spirit directed her to a verse in Isaiah 30 that she had never noticed before. It was verse 15 where the Bible declares, "In quietness and in confidence shall be your strength."

The woman began using half an hour before her family woke up for her quiet time. She began to read God's Word and to consciously consider the love, greatness, and power of God. One morning, on a day which was to be filled with several difficult commitments, she was considering the children of Israel as they crossed the Red Sea. "When I realized how easily God took several million people through that sea," the woman commented, "I knew He could take me safely through any red sea that might arise in my day. I left my quiet time with assurance, confidence, and faith."

Within a short while the woman's nervousness had completely vanished. She soon became such a bulwark of inspiration and strength that people could not believe she had ever been threatened by a nervous breakdown.[1]

Christians today are bombarded by distractions. I am sure that Satan uses everything he can to keep us from simply being quiet before God. Noise pollution takes its toll on all of us. Radios and televisions blare all day long. Telephones seem to ring incessantly. Automobiles and airplanes, machinery of every kind, make us almost numb to the beauty of quietness.

Our mechanized society, with all its labor-saving devices, has actually become more hectic than ever. We are caught up, it seems, in one continuous flurry of activity. And when we finally do set aside a few moments for devotions, we find that our minds are filled with a hundred and one people to see, things to do, and places to go.

And so many Christians go on and on, never seeming to find time to spend with God, and, as a result, rarely enjoying the fruitful, abundant life that Christ offers to us.

The quiet time is not just a helpful idea; it is absolutely necessary to spiritual growth. Just as it is easier to fight off a cold if we are in good physical condition, so it is easier to fight off the devil if we are spiritually fit.

So—no matter who you are—new Christian, old Christian, pastor or layman—you have little hope of living triumphantly unless you seriously maintain your quiet time.

---

1. Louise Smith, "Be Still and Know God," *Christian Life*, May 1961, p. 30.

Isaiah wrote, "Even the young shall faint and be weary, and the young men shall utterly fall: but they that wait upon the LORD shall renew their strength; they shall mount up with wings as eagles; they shall run, and not be weary; and they shall walk, and not faint" (Isaiah 40:30-31).

"All right," you say, "I agree that the quiet time is important, but I have never been successful in keeping one. It doesn't seem to work for me."

HELPFUL SUGGESTIONS

How can we be still and know God in the midst of this high-pressure society? How can we maintain a successful quiet time? Here are some suggestions which I have found to be helpful in my personal life:

1. Recognize the importance of a quiet time.

It is very easy to give lip service to our need for fellowship with God. It is another thing entirely to be personally committed to those words. We are never truly successful at what we do unless we are committed to its achievement.

Borden of Yale expressed his need for this special devotional time: "I have only missed my Quiet Time once or twice this term. . . . I can easily believe that it is next in importance to accepting Christ. For I know that when I do not wait on God in prayer and Bible study, *things go wrong.*"

Because we believe food is necessary to our physical well-being, we eat three times a day. We must feed spiritually for the same reason.

Peter wrote, "As newborn babes, desire the sincere milk of the word, that ye may grow thereby" (1 Peter 2:2).

Martin Luther said that "to be a Christian *without prayer* is no more possible than to be alive without breathing." Communication with Jesus Christ through prayer and through His Word is the spiritual lifeline of every believer.

Jesus Himself spent much time in meditation and prayer. Mark 1:35 reads, "And in the morning, rising up a great while before day, he went out, and departed into a solitary place, and there prayed." If Jesus Christ, who was in perfect harmony with God the Father, withdrew to a solitary place for prayer, how can we do less?

2. *Cultivate a taste for the quiet time.*

Peter challenges us to "desire" the Word of God (1 Peter 2:2). Jeremiah wrote, "Thy words were found, and I did eat them; and thy word was unto me the joy and rejoicing of mine heart" (Jeremiah 15:16).

"How do you eat the Word?" you ask. Well, what happens when you take physical food into your body? That glass of white milk you drink turns into blue eyes and blonde hair. Those green vegetables you eat become part of your white, or brown, or yellow skin. What you digest becomes a part of you.

So the same is to be true as we read and meditate upon God's Word. We are to digest it. It is to become a part of our lives.

We should also desire to talk with God, to be with Him in prayer. Because I love my wife, I want to be with her. I enjoy talking to her. When I am traveling away from home I eagerly look forward to calling her on the phone.

If we sincerely love Jesus Christ, we should have this same desire. We will want to be in contact with Him. For you and me to have fellowship with God is a very wonderful thing. But even more wonderful is the realization that Almighty God seeks our fellowship. John writes that "the Father seeketh such to worship him" (John 4:23). Just think of it, God desires to meet with me! My quiet time is my time alone with God.

3. Determine to maintain the quiet time.

The maintenance of a successful quiet time requires determination and discipline. Seek to avoid all interruptions. Don't let the telephone rob you of your time with God. Arrange your schedule so that you can be alone—totally alone with God—for a specific length of time each day.

"But you don't know my schedule," you say. "You don't know how busy I am."

If you are too busy to maintain a quiet time, I'm afraid you are too busy. I have found that we have time for just about anything that is really important to us. We do that which we really want to do.

What's important to you? If you want to look attractive, you spend the necessary time in front of the mirror. If you enjoy reading, you are likely to spend several hours per day with a book. Civic work, even church work, takes up our time because we are convinced of its importance.

But what about fellowship with God? If we don't maintain a quiet time each day, it's not really because we are too busy; it's because we do not feel it is important enough.

It is said that John Wesley preached over 44,000 sermons in his lifetime. He traveled by horseback and carriage nearly 300,000 miles, wrote grammar and theological textbooks in four languages, and yet always had time for a quiet time. While still in his childhood, Wesley resolved to dedicate an hour each morning and evening to Bible study and prayer. And he kept that vow throughout his lifetime.

Maintaining a daily quiet time is basically a matter of putting first things first. Dorothy Haskin tells the story of a noted concert artist who was asked the secret of her mastery of the violin. "Planned neglect," she replied and then explained, "There were many things which used to demand my time. When I went to my room after breakfast, I made my bed, straightened the room, dusted, and did whatever seemed necessary. When I finished my work, I turned to my violin practice. That system failed, however, to accomplish what I should on the violin, so I reversed things. I deliberately planned to neglect everything else until my practice period was complete. And that program of planned neglect is the secret of my success."[2]

Perhaps there are some things *you* need to neglect so that you can be successful in maintaining your time with God. We must *make time* for fellowship with our heavenly Father. We organize for ev-

---

2. Dorothy Haskin, *A Practical Guide to Prayer* (Chicago: Moody, 1951), p. 32.

erything else, so why not organize for a quiet time?

"Prayer is the key of the morning and the bolt of the evening," said Matthew Henry.

Discipline is required for a faithful, fruitful quiet time.

Practical Steps in Developing the Quiet Time

1. Be regular.

The Christians in the city of Berea "searched the scriptures daily, whether those things were so" (Acts 17:11).

Seek to meet the Lord at the same time and same place each day. A *definite time* and *place* will help a great deal in developing regularity.

Do not attempt to bite off more than you can chew to begin with. To attempt too much to start with can lead to discouragement and failure. It is also wiser to begin with fifteen minutes daily than a few hours once a week. Determine to do only that which you honestly feel you can accomplish each day.

2. Be quiet.

"In quietness and in confidence shall be your strength" (Isaiah 30:15).

Make your quiet time a *quiet time*. "Be still, and know that I am God" (Psalm 46:10). There's an old navy rule: when ships readjust their compass, they drop anchor in a *quiet spot*. Decide where you can find a quiet spot.

If you cannot find a quiet place, then you will have to close the door of your mind to all the surrounding distractions.

More important than finding a quiet spot is a quiet spirit. Open yourself to all that God has for you. William Runyan has expressed it well:

> Lord, I have shut the door, speak now the word
> Which in the din and throng could not be heard;
> Hushed now my inner heart, whisper Thy will,
> While I have come apart, while all is still.[3]

3. Be systematic.

"They received the word with all readiness of mind" (Acts 17:11).

The time you choose for your quiet time is up to you. The great missionary Hudson Taylor used to say, "Whatever is your best time in the day, give that to communion with God." Some people wake up quickly while others wake up slowly. Some of us are roosters and others are owls.

Consistency is the important thing. I have personally found the morning to be the best time for my quiet time with God. The psalmist wrote, "My voice shalt thou hear in the morning, O LORD; in the morning will I direct my prayer unto thee, and look up" (Psalm 5:3). The Lord said, "I love them that love me; and those that seek me early shall find me" (Proverbs 8:17).

If you are like most people, you are probably more alert in the morning than you are just before bedtime. But in order to regularly meet God in the morning you must get to bed at a reasonable time at night. You may have to set your

---

3. William M. Runyan, "Lord, I Have Shut the Door," copyright, 1923. Renewal, 1951, by W. M. Runyan. Assigned to Hope Publishing Company. All rights reserved. Used by permission.

priorities in order. You may have to put that book or magazine down a little earlier. You may have to switch off the TV or radio.

Consistency requires faithfulness. The apostle Paul wrote, "It is required in stewards, that a man be found faithful" (1 Corinthians 4:2). Each one of us is a steward. We have twenty-four hours in every day to spend as we wish. How are you using your time?

When a person receives Jesus Christ as Savior, he becomes a member of the family of God. God becomes our heavenly Father and we become His children. Any good father wants to spend time with his children. This is how we really get to know each other.

I would suggest that the quiet time begin with prayer to God, asking for His blessing on your time together. Prayer is the key that unlocks the treasures of God's Word.

Prayer time should include praise and thanksgiving for all God is doing and will do. Pray for your loved ones. Pray for others. Pray for yourself. It is a thrilling privilege to pray.

After prayer, you'll want to read God's Word, His special message to you. Secure a rather large Bible with print that is easy to read. Small type can be discouraging.

The Lord's formula for Joshua's prosperity and success was: "This book of the law shall not depart out of thy mouth; but thou shalt meditate therein day and night, that thou mayest observe to do according to all that is written therein: for then thou shalt make thy way prosperous, and then thou shalt have good success" (Joshua 1:8).

To meditate is to think quietly and deeply about the greatness and goodness of God. Notice the promises of God. Look for guiding principles for your daily life. Commit to memory a meaningful verse. Don't hurry. Regularly, quietly, systematically, yet leisurely, meditate upon the written Word and the living Word.

4. Be rested.

"I will give thee rest" (Exodus 33:14).

Spiritual rest is a gift from God. However, it is extremely important that we enjoy physical rest. It is difficult physically to get to bed late and get up early. Late nights can kill the quiet time.

5. Be expectant.

"Now unto him that is able to do exceeding abundantly above all that we ask or think, according to the power that worketh in us" (Ephesians 3:20).

Remember, that in order to have a successful quiet time you must expect God to do something for you each day. Pray, expecting Him to answer your prayers. Ask Him to open your mind and heart to His fullness. Read His Word, expecting Him to speak to you—to meet a specific need in your life.

Do you lack power in your life? Does it feel as if there is something missing in your Christian experience? Why not purpose in your heart from this day forward that you will have your quiet time.

Lord, I have shut the door, here do I bow;

> Speak, for my soul attent turns to Thee now.
> Rebuke Thou what is vain, counsel my soul,
> Thy holy will reveal, my will control.
>
> Lord, I have shut the door, strengthen my heart;
> Yonder awaits the task—I share a part.
> Only through grace bestowed may I be true;
> Here, while alone with Thee, my strength renew.[4]
>
> WILLIAM M. RUNYAN

REMINDERS

Quiet time is not just a helpful idea, it is absolutely necessary to spiritual growth.

"To be a Christian without prayer is no more possible than to be alive without breathing."

MARTIN LUTHER

If we don't maintain a quiet time each day, it's not really because we are too busy; it's because we do not feel it is important enough.

There's an old navy rule: when ships readjust their compass, they drop anchor in a quiet spot.

Late nights kill the quiet time.

QUESTIONS

1. What is the quiet time?
2. According to Mark 1:35, what was the example of Jesus in the quiet time?
3. How would you relate Jeremiah 15:16 to a quiet time?

---

4. Ibid.

4. What part does discipline play in cultivating the quiet time?
5. List some practical steps in developing the quiet time.
6. What are the enemies of the quiet time?
7. Why is a definite time and place important?
8. What does it mean to be a "steward" (1 Corinthians 4:2)? How does that relate to our quiet time?
9. What is God's formula for success (Joshua 1:8)?
10. What should we expect God to do in the quiet time?

8
The Three Divisions of Mankind

But the natural man receiveth not the things of the Spirit of God: for they are foolishness unto him: neither can he know them, because they are spiritually discerned. But he that is spiritual judgeth all things, yet he himself is judged of no man.

1 CORINTHIANS 2:14-15

The natural man does not know God. The carnal man does not share God's love with a needy world. It is the spiritual man alone who is motivated and directed by the constraining love of Christ.

* * *

Our world is divided by wealth, education, race, age, and even geography. Some of these divisions are natural and helpful. Others are artificial and harmful.

The Bible divides all of mankind into three groups. These divisions are not according to the measure of our possessions or the color of our skin. In fact, the apostle Paul tells us that in Christ there is "neither Jew nor Greek . . . bond nor free . . . male nor female" (Galatians 3:28).

God's divisions of mankind are based entirely upon the *spiritual condition* of the human heart! In the New Testament book of 1 Corinthians 2:14—3:4, Paul sets forth the three great divisions of mankind.

THE NATURAL MAN

The first division described is that of the natural man. In 1 Corinthians 2:14 we read that "the natural man receiveth not the things of the Spirit of God: for they are foolishness unto him: neither can he know them, because they are spiritually discerned."

Who is the natural man? He is the person who has been born *only once!* He is alive physically, but spiritually dead. He is motivated primarily by his own physical desires. He is unbelieving, unconverted, and unsaved.

Once a religious leader named Nicodemus came to Jesus seeking spiritual guidance. Jesus told him that "except a man be born of water and of the Spirit, he cannot enter into the kingdom of God" (John 3:5). Jesus then defined the natural man. "That which is born of the flesh," said Jesus, "is flesh" (v. 6). The natural man is flesh. Jesus Christ is *not* in the life. Self is supreme. Jesus Christ is excluded.

The natural man is ego-centered. He basically functions and seeks his fulfillment in the five human senses.

Although he may be outwardly very gracious, courteous, and kind, he is inwardly self-centered and seeks primarily to gratify his fleshly desires. His spirit has never been touched by the Holy Spirit, and he is separated from God.

Despite natural gifts and physical accomplishments, the natural man experiences a deep lack in his life. It was Pascal who declared, "There is a God-shaped vacuum in every heart," and only God can fill that. Henry Thoreau, the naturalist author, also admitted, "The mass of men live lives of quiet desperation!"

The first great division of mankind is the natural man. To the natural man the things of God are foreign and contrary. Paul tells us that he is unable to comprehend the things of God, he can't tune in, he has no equipment or aptitude for measuring divine truth. The natural man is on a completely different wavelength; he operates on a different level.

The Bible goes on to tell us that the natural man does not understand the things of God. Why? Because "they are foolishness unto him" (1 Corinthians 2:14). The word *foolish* comes from the Greek adjective *moros,* meaning dull, tasteless, and insipid. In other words, spiritual matters are distasteful and even absurd to the man without Jesus Christ.

Not only are the things of God foolishness to the natural man, but the Scriptures continue, "Neither can he know them" (1 Corinthians 2:14). It is not just that he does not know; he *cannot* know the things of God because "they are spiritually discerned" (1 Corinthians 2:14).

A young college professor once said to me, "Dr.

Sweeting, I've tried to read the Bible a hundred times. It just doesn't add up. I was reared in a fine home. I even have a brother who is a minister; but for some reason, I just can't seem to understand it."

My friend, this is no mystery. Paul said, "Neither can he know the things of God," for man in his unconverted state is governed by his fleshly nature.

THE CARNAL MAN

The second major division of mankind is that of the *carnal man*. The natural man is one totally alienated from God, whereas the carnal man is a Christian under fleshly control. He has experienced *God's salvation* but he is not experiencing *God's sovereignty.* He has been born physically and spiritually. Christ is in the life, but self is still supreme! Ego still sits in the driver's seat.

In 1 Corinthians 3:1, Paul tells the believers at Corinth that he was forced to speak to them as "carnal, even as unto babes in Christ."

Now, of course, there is nothing wrong with being a spiritual baby. That's where we all begin. Peter, speaking to new Christians, writes, "As newborn babes, desire the sincere milk of the word, that ye may grow thereby" (1 Peter 2:2). We all must start our Christian experience as infants—as newborn babes.

But the tragedy occurs when a person *remains* an infantile Christian. A mother is understandably alarmed if her baby fails to develop normally. A farmer is financially ruined if his crops do not grow and bring forth fruit. The first law of life is expansion. Without growth there can *be* no life!

Why is it important that we grow as Christians? Because it is God's plan for us. In Romans 8:29 we read that "whom he did foreknow, he also did predestinate to be conformed to the image of his Son." God desires that we be made like unto Jesus Christ. Wretched and miserable is the Christian who resists God's plan for development.

Let's look for a moment at the characteristics of the carnal man. Like an infant, he is easily offended and hurt. The small baby will cry at the slightest provocation. Any unusual activity is likely to disturb him. The carnal Christian is shortsighted. As with the young child, he lacks judgment and is immature. As these characteristics are normal for the child, they are also normal for the young Christian. It is only as the Christian fails to grow that carnality expresses itself. Unfortunately, many Christians remain spiritual infants throughout their lives. Their growth has been arrested and stunted.

Envy, strife, and divisions are characteristics of the carnal man. In 1 Corinthians 3:3 Paul says, "For whereas there is among you envying, and strife, and divisions, are ye not carnal, and walk as men?" Children often quarrel and fight. They are impatient and lack self-control. Many times they are unable to get along with one another.

It was carnal Christians who caused many of the problems in the New Testament church. Much of Paul's time and many of his letters were devoted to clearing the confusion and strife created by carnal believers. Why? Because although Jesus Christ was in their lives, He was not supreme. They were more concerned with the physical than they were with the spiritual issues of life. They did not know the centrality and sufficiency of Jesus Christ.

My friend, where do you stand today? Are you growing? Is your spiritual life fruitful or unfruitful? Are you a carnal Christian—saved yet so as by fire? The carnal man is the second division of mankind—converted, but ruled by self.

THE SPIRITUAL MAN

In 1 Corinthians 2:15-16, Paul speaks of the third great division of mankind. Here he presents a picture of *the spiritual man*. "He that is spiritual," says Paul, "judgeth all things, yet he himself is judged of no man. For who hath known the mind of the Lord, that he may instruct him? But we have the mind of Christ."

Who is the spiritual man? Paul is not speaking of the rank and file of believers. The spiritual man is certainly a believer; but more than that, he is one whose life is controlled by the Holy Spirit of God. Jesus Christ is not only *in* his life, but He is *in control* of his life! He has experienced the second birth, and Jesus Christ is *Lord*. Jesus Christ reigns and rules.

The apostle Paul was a spiritual man. To the believers of Galatia he wrote, "I am crucified with Christ: nevertheless I live; yet not I, but Christ liveth in me: and the life which I now live in the flesh I live by the faith of the Son of God" (Galatians 2:20).

The spiritual man is the man who has totally

committed himself to Jesus Christ. Jesus Christ is supreme in his life. In contrast to the immaturity of the carnal man, the spiritual man is one who grows in the things of God and brings forth fruit.

The spiritual man is one who has experienced the love of God and who in turn is desirous of sharing that love with others.

The natural man *does not know God.* The carnal man *does not share God's love* with a needy world. It is the spiritual man alone who is motivated and directed by the constraining love of Christ.

According to 1 Corinthians 2:15, we find that the spiritual man is given *discernment.* The *spiritual man* is able to make right decisions, he is able to understand the Scriptures and to live in God's perfect will.

"He that is spiritual," says Paul, "judgeth [or discerneth] all things, yet he himself is judged of no man" (1 Corinthians 2:15).

Finally, the spiritual man is one who displays *the mind of Christ.* Paul instructed believers at Philippi to "let this mind be in you, which was also in Christ Jesus" (Philippians 2:5). The spiritual man is characterized by the mind of Christ, a mind of service and submission. He displays the mind of one who "made himself of no reputation, and took upon him the form of a servant, and . . . humbled himself, and became obedient unto death, even the death of the cross" (2:7-8).

In an Italian city stands a statue of a Grecian maiden with a beautiful face, graceful figure, and noble expression. One day a poor little peasant girl came face to face with the statue. She stood and

The Three Divisions of Mankind

stared, and then went home to wash her face and comb her hair. The next day she came again to stand before the statue, and then to return home once more. This time she mended her tattered clothing. Day by day she changed, her form grew more graceful, and her face more refined, till she greatly reflected the famous statue. She was transformed in appearance!

Just so, the spiritual man must each day seek to conform to the perfect image of our Lord and Savior Jesus Christ. Are you more like Jesus Christ today than a month ago?

There are three divisions of mankind: *natural*, *carnal* and *spiritual*. In which category are you, my friend?

If you are still a natural man, you can become a spiritual man by acknowledging your sin and receiving Jesus Christ as your personal Savior.

Perhaps you are a carnal man. You, too, can become a spiritual Christian right now by yielding your life totally to Jesus Christ, by acknowledging your self-centeredness, and by making Jesus Christ *supreme*.

How? The Bible says that "if we confess our sins, he is faithful and just to forgive us our sins, and to cleanse us from all unrighteousness" (1 John 1:9).

REMINDERS

God's divisions of mankind are based entirely upon the spiritual condition of the human heart!

The Basics of the Christian Life

> "The mass of men live lives of quiet desperation."
>
> HENRY THOREAU
>
> The *natural man* is ego-centered. He basically functions and seeks his fulfillment in the five human senses.
>
> The *natural man* is one totally alienated from God, whereas the *carnal man* is a Christian under fleshly control.
>
> The *spiritual man* is able to make right decisions, he is able to understand the Scriptures and to live in God's perfect will.

QUESTIONS

1. Who is the natural man according to 1 Corinthians 2:14?
2. Why are the things of God meaningless to the natural man, according to 1 Corinthians 2:14?
3. Who is the carnal man?
4. List three characteristics of the carnal man according to 1 Corinthians 3:3.
5. Who is the spiritual man?
6. List two qualities of the spiritual man according to 1 Corinthians 2:15.
7. Why do Christians allow themselves to live in a carnal condition?
8. What is discernment? Why does only the spiritual man have it?
9. How can we "conform" ourselves to Christ (Romans 8:29)?
10. In which division of mankind are you?

9
How to Be Sure of Salvation

> *These things have I written unto you that believe on the name of the Son of God; that ye may know that ye have eternal life, and that ye may believe on the name of the Son of God.*
>
> 1 JOHN 5:13

> It is the rightful heritage of every believer, even the newest in the family of faith, to be absolutely certain that eternal life is his present possession. To look to self is to tremble. To look to Calvary's finished work is to triumph.
>
> LARRY McGUILL

* * *

"Can I really be sure of salvation?"

That was a question asked recently by a young man overcome by doubt. He had lost all the peace he once knew, and was now searching desperately for some word of hope.

The Bible tells us that we can know—beyond a shadow of a doubt—that we are God's children.

Assurance of salvation can be yours right now in this life.

It's shocking to realize how many people are made miserable by the disease called doubt. Uncertainty has robbed thousands of people of the joy of salvation.

People who even read their Bibles, earnestly pray, faithfully attend church, and live uprightly in all their dealings with others, may yet have no assurance of forgiveness and be living defeated lives.

Is assurance of salvation possible? What does the Bible say? In 2 Corinthians 13:5, Paul writes, "Examine yourselves, whether ye be in the faith." In 2 Peter 1:10 we are told, "Give diligence to make your calling and election sure." The assurance of salvation is one of God's beautiful gifts. Every believer ought to know that he possesses salvation.

Assurance is not only possible but necessary because it is that reality which brings purpose and power to our lives. Christian assurance is a fortress of strength against the wiles of the devil. An uncertain salvation is a sad one which repels rather than attracts others. Assurance adds zeal and vitality to Christian service.

Don't waste years in doubt; move forward to enjoy the greater things of God. Assurance is not necessary for salvation, but it's necessary for an overcoming life.

What does the word *assurance* actually mean? Assurance for the Christian is "the unwavering confidence of an intelligent faith in a present salvation." Having this knowledge is not only the privilege but the duty of every believer.

KNOWING BY THE WORD OF GOD

"How can I have this assurance?" you ask. We must begin with the Bible. Assurance of salvation is based upon acceptance of the Bible as the unerring Word of God. As we apply the promises of the Bible to our lives, doubt leaves.

A Bible illustration of this truth is given to us in the life of Abraham. Abraham received a promise from God that was humanly impossible, yet the Bible says, "He staggered not at the promise of God through unbelief" (Romans 4:20). We are also told that "Abraham believed God, and it was accounted to him for righteousness" (Galatians 3:6). The promises of God are as sure as God is.

The apostle John knew the difficulties of doubt. He saw many groping yet never finding, wishing but still waiting, looking yet still longing because of doubt. "These things have I written unto you that believe on the name of the Son of God; that ye may know that ye have eternal life, and that ye may believe on the name of the Son of God" (1 John 5:13). The object is that "ye may know that ye have eternal life." The word *know* means "to recognize the quality of." The apostle John wrote these verses so that we might recognize the quality of our position in Christ. This is not an opinion or a matter of inference but a revelation from God. Assurance is based upon the truthfulness of God. Failure to believe is to make God a liar.

My friend, trust God and fear will flee, conscience will be calmed. Your heart will be at rest.

Imagine a prisoner being offered a pardon. He reads the official document but is so overwhelmed that he is dazed by the news. Suppose you ask, "Have you been pardoned?" He would say, "Yes." You might ask, "Do you feel pardoned?" He replies, "No, I do not; it is so sudden." "But," you ask, "if you do not feel pardoned, how can you know you are?" "Oh," he says, as he points to the document, "This tells me so." The Bible is God's document of pardon to every believer.

COMMON MISCONCEPTIONS

Often there are misconceptions which make some Christians believe that assurance is impossible. A salesman friend recently said to me, "But I cannot know I am the Lord's till the day I die. It's presumptuous to be so certain."

I assured him that assurance is not arrogant presumption, but a humble knowledge of present acceptance by God. This confidence is based on the finished work of Christ. It is not self-confidence, for the Scripture says, "Not by works of righteousness which we have done, but according to his mercy he saved us" (Titus 3:5). My friend, is it presumptuous to accept what God has said?

The Philippian jailer called out, "What must I do to be saved?" (Acts 16:30). Paul answered, "Believe on the Lord Jesus Christ, and thou shalt be saved"

(v. 31). The Philippian jailer believed and was converted! Is it presumptuous to believe God?

You ask, "What if I'm not one of the elect?" Jesus said, "Whosoever believeth . . . should not perish, but have everlasting life" (John 3:16). This includes you! Salvation is offered to all. The Bible says that all men are sinners, and if we call upon the Lord we shall be saved. Dwight L. Moody used to say, "The elect are the 'whosoever wills'; the non-elect are the 'whosoever won'ts.' " Assurance is not the prerogative of a select few, but of all God's people.

Others think they must know the day and the hour of their decision. This is wonderful to know, but not necessary. A dear friend of mine was very concerned because she could not recall the exact time of her conversion. She was sure that she had received Christ as Savior and Lord but she didn't know when. I assured her that her assurance of salvation was more important than knowing the exact date she was saved. "But," you say, "if you don't know the date, how can you be sure?"

May I ask, "How do you know you are alive physically?" "Oh," you say, "I breathe, I eat, I think, I resolve."

So it is spiritually; if you have been converted, you will be interested in spiritual matters, you will breathe the atmosphere of heaven by praying, you will read the Bible, and you will be faithful in the local church where God has placed you. Should it be that your life is no different from the unconverted, then perhaps you have never been converted.

Then there are others who believe they must go

through the valley of terror and tears before they can know. Tears which result in genuine repentance are beautiful, but mere tears of remorse cannot avail.

Our salvation rests upon fact. The Bible says, "I delivered unto you first of all that which I also received, how that Christ died for our sins according to the scriptures; and that he was buried, and that he rose again the third day according to the scriptures" (1 Corinthians 15:3-4). These are the facts. After facts comes faith, and then feelings. Many people completely lack assurance because they fail to realize a very important point: faith brings assurance!

KNOWING BY THE WITNESS WITHIN

Assurance of salvation is possible by the witness of the Holy Spirit. At your conversion, you became the dwelling place of the Holy Spirit. This heavenly Guest wants complete lordship of your life. Yielding to the Holy Spirit brings definite assurance. Many, through carelessness and lack of knowledge, grieve the Holy Spirit and know little or nothing of the witness within. Paul the apostle said, "Ye have received the Spirit of adoption, whereby we cry, Abba, Father. The Spirit itself beareth witness with our spirit, that we are the children of God: and if children, then heirs; heirs of God, and joint-heirs with Christ" (Romans 8:15-17). What solid certainty this provides! Since God is our Father and we are His children, we cry, "Abba, Father," or literally, "My own dear Father." The cry is born of the Holy Spirit.

How to Be Sure of Salvation

A. T. Pierson said, "When a child begins to talk, he uses the simplest consonants and the simplest vowels; and because he knows how to make but one syllable, he repeats the syllable. And so he says, 'papa' and 'mama.' The word for 'abba' is Aramaic for our word *papa*." Slavish fear is replaced with childlike love and the spirit of adoption rather than bondage. There is a father-child relationship, and we are in the family of God. Earthly parents are hurt by the mistrust of a child, and so doubt grieves the heart of God. Assurance rests primarily in the promises of God's Word, then subjectively in the experience of the believer. There is a danger here in making the experience of others the way for all.

The witness of the Spirit is the testimony of the indwelling Holy Spirit with our spirit, that we are the children of God. The Holy Spirit opens our eyes to eternal values, lightens our minds to perceive the truth, fills our hearts with divine love, gives compassion for others, makes intercession for us when we know not how to pray, comforts in the hours of tears, strengthens in the midst of battle, lifts us in the vale of defeat. These are some of the works of the Spirit in the believer. The Word of God says, "But the fruit of the Spirit is love, joy, peace, longsuffering, gentleness, goodness, faith, meekness, temperance" (Galatians 5:22-23). If the fruit of the Spirit is in evidence, you may be sure of God's gracious work in your life.

A soldier lay dying on the battlefield. The chaplain asked, "What church are you of?"

"Of the church of Christ," he replied.

"I mean, what persuasion are you?"

"Persuasion!" said the wounded soldier as he looked upward. "I am persuaded, that neither death, nor life, nor angels nor principalities, nor powers, nor things present, nor things to come, nor height, nor depth, nor any other creature, shall be able to separate us from the love of God, which is in Christ Jesus our Lord" (Romans 8:38-39).

At the conclusion of a mass meeting, I was greeting people when a distinguished-looking man approached me and asked, "May I talk with you about my salvation? I'm desperately confused." He went on to state that he had acknowledged the Lord as Savior but had little peace and Christian confidence. "As I listened to your message, I decided I must settle it."

I replied. "First, look into your life to discover if all is right between yourself and the Lord. Carnal believers are usually full of doubts. If the Holy Spirit is grieved through self-will or sin, He cannot witness effectively to your salvation because there is contradiction. For this reason the witness of the Holy Spirit is often dimmed. Second, after discovering the wrong, openly confess it to the Lord. Third, deal with it and do works to prove your repentance."

"That's it," he interrupted. "I've grown careless; there's sin in my life, and I must make it right."

We bowed our heads in a holy hush as he sought God's gracious forgiveness. It was evident that the Lord was in the room, for when we arose from our knees the doctor was changed. His expression, his voice, his whole attitude radiated blessed assurance. Careless living will always create doubt, but the opposite is also true. Doubt leads to careless living.

You will recall the story of Moses climbing Mount Sinai to receive the law. When he failed to return, the Israelites complained to Aaron, asking for Moses. Because Moses did not return, they doubted. On the heels of doubt followed sinful suggestions, and soon the Israelites danced around the golden calf. *Sinful living dims the witness of the Holy Spirit.*

KNOWING BY THE WORKS OF YOUR LIFE

Assurance of salvation is based upon the fruit of one's life. Let's look at some Bible tests.

1. Obedience

The first test is obedience. "And hereby we do know that we know him, if we keep his commandments. He that saith, I know him, and keepeth not his commandments, is a liar, and the truth is not in him" (1 John 2:3-4).

Do you obey the Word of God? Jesus said, "If ye love me, keep my commandments" (John 14:15). "And why call ye me, Lord, Lord, and do not the things which I say?" (Luke 6:46).

Is it your ambition to do the works of Christ? Do you delight in the law of the Lord? Are you a "doer of the Word"? Constant assurance depends upon practical obedience to the Word of God. Obedience is a good test, for Jesus said, "My sheep hear my voice, and I know them, and they follow me"

(John 10:27). Again, "He that . . . worketh righteousness, is accepted" (Acts 10:35).

2. *Love for the brethren*

Do you possess Christian love? A love for God's people is evidence of personal salvation. "He that saith he is in the light, and hateth his brother, is in darkness even until now" (1 John 2:9). "For this is the message that ye heard from the beginning, that we should love one another. Not as Cain, who was of that wicked one, and slew his brother. And wherefore slew he him? Because his own works were evil, and his brother's righteous" (1 John 3:11-12). Many professing Christians are destitute of love for others. Are you following Cain or Christ? The love test is important. Perhaps at times you are not too sure you love the Lord. May I ask, "Do you love your mother?"

"Yes," you say.

"Well, how do you know?"

You say, "I show it by my affection and the things I do for her." So also you may know whether you love the Lord by the things you do for Him. The natural man is at odds with God. "Every one that loveth is born of God" (1 John 4:7). Do you love fellow believers? "We know that we have passed from death unto life, because we love the brethren. He that loveth not his brother abideth in death" (1 John 3:14). "By this shall all men know that ye are my disciples, if ye have love one to another" (John 13:35).

3. *Love for God's Word*

Do you love God's Word? David said, "The statutes of the LORD are right, rejoicing the heart: the commandment of the LORD is pure, enlightening the eyes. The fear of the LORD is clean, enduring for ever: the judgments of the LORD are true and righteous altogether. More to be desired are they than gold, yea, than much fine gold: sweeter also than honey and the honeycomb" (Psalm 19:8-10).

4. *Desire to worship*

Do you love God's house? "I was glad when they said unto me, Let us go into the house of the LORD" (Psalm 122:1).

5. *Fruit of the Spirit*

Do you have the fruit of the Spirit? "The fruit of the Spirit is love, joy, peace, longsuffering, gentleness, goodness, faith, meekness, temperance: against such there is no law" (Galatians 5:22).

After the apostle Paul met Christ, his life was proof of conversion. Love is difficult to hide. When a young man is in love, it is obvious. The same applies in the spiritual realm. Ask yourself again, "Do I love the Lord? Do I love His people? Do I love the Bible? Do I love to pray? Do I love God's house?" Your answer will help you to know where you stand.

All of us at times have passed through the sea of doubt. Bunyan speaks of being "much tumbled up and down in his thoughts." However, without question we may know now that we have eternal life. Jesus said, "He that believeth on me hath everlasting life" (John 6:47). Anything that contradicts the words of Jesus is a lie. "Let God be true, but every man a liar" (Romans 3:4).

Abraham, in the face of the unknown, had complete assurance. "By faith Abraham, when he was called to go out into a place which he should after receive for an inheritance, obeyed; and he went out, not knowing whither he went. By faith he sojourned in the land of promise, as in a strange country, dwelling in tabernacles with Isaac and Jacob, the heirs with him of the same promise: for he looked for a city which hath foundations, whose builder and maker is God" (Hebrews 11:8-10).

David had full assurance. "I will behold thy face in righteousness" (Psalm 17:15).

Daniel had glad assurance. "The people that do know their God shall be strong, and do exploits" (Daniel 11:32).

Job had blessed assurance. "I know that my redeemer liveth" (Job 19:25).

Paul had abundant assurance. "For I know whom I have believed, and am persuaded that he is able to keep that which I have committed unto him against that day" (2 Timothy 1:12).

John the apostle believed in a know-so salvation. "These things have I written unto you that believe on the name of the Son of God; that ye may know that ye have eternal life" (2 John 5:13).

Millions have known this blessed assurance.

When that great Christian scientist Sir Michael Faraday was dying, some journalists questioned him as to his speculations concerning the soul and death. "Speculations!" said the dying man in astonishment. "I know nothing about speculations; I'm resting on certainties. 'I know whom I have believed, and am persuaded that he is able to keep that which I have committed unto him against that day' " (2 Timothy 1:12).

REMINDERS

Assurance for the Christian is "the unwavering confidence of an intelligent faith in a present salvation."

Assurance is based upon the truthfulness of God. Failure to believe is to make God a liar.

Yielding to the Holy Spirit brings definite assurance.

Sinful living dims the witness of the Holy Spirit.

Constant assurance depends upon practical obedience to the Word of God.

QUESTIONS

1. Is assurance of salvation possible? List two verses of Scripture to verify your answer.
2. What do we mean by the word *assurance?*
3. Can we possess assurance of salvation according to 1 John 5:13?
4. List four misconceptions regarding the assurance of salvation.
5. What do we mean by the witness of the Holy Spirit?
6. Is there a relationship of obedience to the witness of the Holy Spirit?
7. Assurance of salvation will be seen in at least four areas. What are they?

8. Why do some people think certainty of salvation is impossible?
9. How does sin affect our ability to have assurance?
10. What is the "fruit of the Spirit" (Galatians 5:22)? How do you get it?

10

Worldliness and You

Love not the world, neither the things that are in the world. If any man love the world, the love of the Father is not in him.

1 JOHN 2:15

At the moment of conversion, the Holy Spirit comes to dwell within you. His presence assures you of a living Guide. He will help you evaluate your life according to God's will.

* * *

A favorite feature in *The Reader's Digest,* almost since its beginning, has been its articles recalling "My Most Unforgettable Character."

Sometimes well-known persons have been highlighted, but far more frequently these features have pointed to little-known men and women. They have been persons whose lives mattered in some special way because of their characters, their personalities, or of what they meant to others.

The true Christian is an *unforgettable character*

who, day after day, is becoming more and more like the most unforgettable Person the world has ever known. I speak, of course, of *Jesus Christ*.

The Christian life is not a matter of following a certain list of "dos" or observing a longer list of "don'ts." *The Christian life is a positive allegiance to Jesus Christ.* It is becoming so occupied with Him that the values and standards of the world around have little influence. If you have been born again, if you have trusted Jesus Christ as your personal Savior, you have experienced a wonderful transformation. You are a new creature. You have a brand-new nature. You belong to a new and different kind of family.

As a result, you have an entirely new outlook. A new destination is now yours. Your whole attitude is different.

During the Middle Ages, the Separatists believed it was impossible to live a holy life unless they were isolated from the world about them. Their answer was to build communities walled off from the society they had tried to leave behind. As the years would pass, however, the evils of civilization would move in upon them and a new start would seem necessary.

Escape from the world is really impossible. Nor should we want to escape. God wants us in the world for a holy purpose—to be witnesses for Jesus Christ.

That is our only real excuse for living in this world. And we cannot be what God intended unless we let Him keep us different.

What Is Separation?

The Bible speaks of separation. For example, the apostle Paul plainly instructed Christians at Corinth against involvement with the world around them. "Be ye not unequally yoked together with unbelievers," he wrote in 2 Corinthians 6:14.

Like our society today, Corinth was wicked. The very name *Corinthian* became synonymous with lustful conduct. Even religious worship included immoral exhibitions.

With fatherly concern, the apostle wrote, "Come out from among them, and be ye separate, saith the Lord" (2 Corinthians 6:17). We are *in* the world, but surely not *of* the world.

When the apostle tells us not to be yoked with unbelievers, he is referring to passages like Deuteronomy 22:9-11. Here we find the command "Thou shalt not sow thy vineyard with divers seeds: lest the fruit of thy seed which thou hast sown, and the fruit of thy vineyard, be defiled. Thou shalt not plow with an ox and an ass together. Thou shalt not wear a garment of divers sorts, as of woolen and linen together."

The principle here is simply this: What God has joined, we must not separate; and what He has separated, we must not join.

Why does the Bible forbid unequal yoking? Because it is *unfitting* and *unfair*. The ox and the ass were different in size, temperament, and strength. The ox was considered clean; the ass was an unclean animal. Both would have suffered discomfort and pain from unequal yoking. Harnessing them together would have formed a *poor working combination*.

The great Greek scholar A. T. Robertson translated the passage about unequal yoking this way: "Stop becoming yoked together with the unconverted." J. Henry Jowett said, "Worldliness is a spirit, a temperament, and attitude of the soul. It is a life without high callings, life devoid of lofty ideals. It is a gaze always horizontal and never vertical."

Paul the apostle gets to the heart of the matter in Romans 6:11: "Likewise reckon ye also yourselves to be dead indeed unto sin, but alive unto God through Jesus Christ our Lord."

This is the answer for Christian victory. Count yourself dead to sin and alive to God. Until you do this, the Christian life will be most difficult and confusing.

DEFINITE COMMANDS FOR SEPARATION

But what is a Christian *to do* and what is he *not to do*? The Word of God includes many definite commands. Certain things are always right for the Christian. And certain things are always wrong.

It is always right to be motivated by love for God and a needy world, but it is always wrong to lie, to deceive, or to be governed by evil motives.

Between the definite commands concerning good and evil there is a definite no-man's land that at times presents a problem.

The Bible does not say "Thou shalt" or "Thou

shalt not" concerning certain questions. In this realm, we need the Holy Spirit to apply the principles of the Bible.

At the moment of conversion, the Holy Spirit comes to dwell within you. His presence assures you of a living Guide. He will help you evaluate your life according to God's will. However, always remember that our natures, at best, are very deceitful. In the face of doubt, it is necessary to call for help.

Often I have prayed, "Dear Lord, I am but a little child. Help me to think right. Reveal Thy will. Deliver me from evil and even *the appearance* of evil. Teach me to live in such a way that my conduct will glorify Thee." We need the Holy Spirit's help and we need to pray. But let me also give you some specific guidelines.

BIBLE GUIDELINES FOR SEPARATION

1. Keep in mind the principle of ownership.

We who believe in Jesus Christ have become God's children. We are *twice* His, in fact. He is our *Maker* and also our *Redeemer*. He has *created us* and then He has *purchased us*. Paul asks in 1 Corinthians 6:19, "What? Know ye not that your body is the temple of the Holy Ghost which is in you, which ye have of God, and ye are not your own?"

He then goes on to explain, "For ye are bought with a price: therefore glorify God in your body, and in your spirit, which are God's." We do not belong to ourselves: God created us and redeemed us. Always remember the guideline of ownership.

2. Our conduct as Christians should be governed by our awareness of responsibility for others.

We should ask ourselves, "How will my conduct affect those around me? Am I a stepping-stone or am I a stumbling block?" Never forget that the world knows that the Christian is different. It was because of this principle that Paul wrote in 1 Corinthians 8:13, "Wherefore, if meat make my brother to offend, I will eat no flesh while the world standeth, lest I make my brother to offend." The great apostle was determined to be a good and helpful example to *others*.

The meat offered to the idols was probably the finest meat that money could buy. After it had been offered, it could be purchased cheaply in the open marketplace. But if eating this meat would offend others, Paul would refuse it. We must ask, "How will my conduct affect others?"

3. Keep in mind the effect of your choices on yourself.

This standard centers about your ability to count for God. We should ask, "Will my involvement make me more useful to God, or will it make me less useful? Can I ask His blessing upon my conduct?"

Paul's application of this principle can be seen in 1 Corinthians 9:27, where he says, "But I keep under my body, and bring it into subjection: lest that by any means, when I have preached to others, I myself should be a castaway." Never forget the guideline of *self*. What will my involvement do to my personal effectiveness for God?

Worldliness and You

4. Whatever we do should always be to the glory of God.

This is the all-important test. Always ask, "Can I do this for the glory of God?" Or, "What would Jesus Christ have me do?"

The great apostle sums up this principle in 1 Corinthians 10:31: "Whether therefore ye eat, or drink, or whatsoever ye do, do all to the glory of God." The glory of God should be our supreme desire.

The Bible offers much help in discerning God's will in doubtful areas. 1 Thessalonians 5:22 sets forth a basic guideline, "Abstain from *all* appearance of evil."

Another is found in Romans 12:2: "And be not conformed to this world: but be ye transformed by the renewing of your mind, that ye may prove what is that good, and acceptable, and perfect, will of God." We are to be *transformers* and not *conformers*.

God's will is also mentioned in Galatians 1:4, which speaks of Christ "who gave himself for our sins, that he might deliver us from this present evil world, according to the will of God and our Father."

Ephesians 6:12 describes our opposition: "For we wrestle not against flesh and blood, but against principalities, against powers, against the rulers of the darkness of this world, against spiritual wickedness in high places."

James warns us in his epistle: "Ye adulterers and adulteresses, know ye not that the friendship of the world is enmity with God?" And then he adds,

"Whosoever therefore will be a friend of the world is the enemy of God" (James 4:4).

The apostle John, in his gentle way, gives a parallel warning in 1 John 2:15: "Love not the world, neither the things that are in the world. If any man love the world, the love of the Father is not in him."

The person who is fully yielded to Jesus Christ will have no serious problems with worldliness. May God help you to determine to live victoriously in this world for Christ.

Paul wrote in Galatians 2:20, "I am crucified with Christ: nevertheless I live; yet not I, but Christ liveth in me." In the final analysis, this moment-by-moment experience of letting Christ live in and through us is the answer to living a clearcut Christian life.

REMINDERS

Escape from the world is really impossible. Nor should we want to escape. God wants us in the world for a holy purpose: to be witnesses for Jesus Christ.

The Christian life is a positive allegiance to Jesus Christ. It is becoming so occupied with Him that the values and standards of the world around us have little influence.

"Worldliness is a spirit, a temperament, an attitude of soul. It is a life without callings, life devoid of lofty ideals. It is a gaze always horizontal and never vertical."

JOHN HENRY JOWETT

Worldliness and You

> Never forget that the world knows that the Christian is different.
>
> The person who is fully yielded to Jesus Christ will have no serious problems with worldliness.

QUESTIONS

1. When Paul tells us in 2 Corinthians 6:14 not to be yoked with unbelievers, to which Old Testament passage is he referring?
2. Why does God forbid unequal yoking in Deuteronomy 22:10?
3. When the Bible does not clearly say "thou shalt" or "thou shalt not," how are we to know what is of God?
4. Why do some groups think they must separate themselves physically from the world?
5. List four guidelines for separation and the appropriate Scripture verses.
6. Why did Paul bring his body into subjection?
7. What is the all-important test?
8. What are our responsibilities to others?

11
You and the Church

Ye also, as living stones, are built up a spiritual house.

1 Peter 2:5

The Bible knows nothing of solitary religion.
John Wesley

Men may not read the gospel in seal-skin, or the gospel in morocco, or the gospel in cloth covers but they can't get away from the gospel in shoe leather.

Donald Grey Barnhouse

Church attendance is as vital to a disciple as a transfusion of rich, healthy blood to a sick man.
Dwight L. Moody

* * *

You Need the Church and the Church Needs You

The Bible says we are living stones, joined to one another in God's building. For real success in the

Christian life, every convert, and for that matter, every Christian, needs the fellowship of the church, a divine, permanent institution of which Jesus said, "The gates of hell shall not prevail against it" (Matthew 16:18).

Someone has said, "Though the church has many critics, it has no rivals."

And despite the turmoil and tribulation it may go through, despite the neglect it may receive, the church will remain. It will survive every onslaught and every attack because it is God's institution.

Why Is the Church Important?

The church is important because it is the organization of God, built upon the foundation of Jesus Christ. And, my friend, it will never pass away. It cannot be destroyed.

Jesus Christ is the foundation of the church. In Ephesians 1:22-23, we are told that God the Father has exalted Christ Jesus "and hath put all things under his feet, and gave him to be the head over all things to the church, which is his body, the fulness of him that filleth all in all."

The apostle Paul, in writing to the church at Corinth, emphasized the importance of this fact: "For other foundation can no man lay than that is laid, which is Jesus Christ" (1 Corinthians 3:11). He instructed the believers at Ephesus that the proper love relationship between husband and wife should compare to the relationship of Christ to His church (see Ephesians 5:22-25).

One of the problems of the church is that it is

made up of people like you and me. The church is a divine institution founded by Jesus, but it is also a human institution. It is not a hothouse operating under ideal conditions in a controlled atmosphere. It is an organized group of imperfect saints, all of whom have faults and weaknesses.

We admit our faults, and we want to correct our weaknesses. But there is nothing God has given us, in earth or heaven, no organization that is more meaningful than the church.

WHAT IS THE CHURCH?

I am sure that when many people hear the word *church* they immediately think of a red-brick structure with a tall, impressive steeple. But the Bible never speaks of the church in this regard.

Actually, the Greek word *ekklesia*, which is translated "church" in the New Testament, refers to either a local assembly of Christian believers or else to the universal Body of Christ made up of all people everywhere who have received Jesus Christ as Savior. In 1 Corinthians 1:2 we read, ". . . all that in every place call upon the name of Jesus Christ our Lord." This refers to the *mystical Body* of Christ, often called the *Bride of Christ,* or the church universal. However, this same verse begins, "Unto the church of God which is at Corinth." This plainly refers to *the local congregation* of believers at Corinth.

The word *ekklesia* is made up of two separate words, the preposition *ek* meaning, "out of," and the verb *kaleo,* meaning "to call." The church is *a called-out group of people*, a people separated by God unto Himself.

The English word *church* probably came from the Scottish word *kirk* or the German *kirche*. These, in turn, originated from the Greek word *kuriakon*. This word was used by the Greek Christians to designate a place of worship. It comes from the Greek word *Lord* and means that which is the Lord's place or the Lord's house.

When the word *ekklesia* or *church* is found in the New Testament, it generally refers to a body of believers banded together in a definite place; in other words, a particular group of people organized in a local community, accepting the Scriptures as the basis of faith and conduct.

P. T. Forsythe spoke of the local church as the "outcrop of the church universal." The local church is vital and is God's means of accomplishing His work here on earth.

A friend once told me, "I don't belong to a specific local church because I don't see that commanded in the Bible." But if that friend had studied his Bible at all, he would have realized that the local assembly is strongly emphasized throughout the New Testament. The book of Acts infers that on the day of Pentecost 3,000 new believers were added to the church in Jerusalem. Later on in the book of Acts, we read that the local church in Antioch commissioned Paul and Barnabas and sent them out as missionaries.

The apostle John received seven messages from the Lord Himself directed to seven *local churches*. Paul and his companions spent many years in the work of establishing and encouraging *local assemblies*. Nine of the thirteen epistles which he wrote under the direction of the Holy Spirit were addressed to *local churches*.

In our day it is the local church that sets apart missionaries and supports them. It is the local church that operates Sunday schools, helps the poor, conducts services for worship, edification, and evangelism. It is the local church which serves as the human instrument to perform God's work here on earth. And it is because God's work must and will go on that there is a future for the church of Jesus Christ.

The Apostolic Church

Chapter 2 of the book of Acts vividly relates the story of that first church in Jerusalem. How the Holy Spirit was poured out! In Acts 2:41 we read, "Then they that gladly received his word were baptized: and the same day there were added *unto them* about three thousand souls."

Those early believers *gladly received the Word of God*. They agreed with the Bible's indictment of guilt and sin, and they had an experience with the living Christ. And as a result of this salvation experience, they become a part of the Body of Christ, the church.

Christians down through the centuries have found that it is necessary to have fellowship together. The writer of Hebrews speaks of this when he states, "Not forsaking the assembling of ourselves together, as the manner of some is" (Hebrews

10:25). Martin Luther put it this way: "To gather with God's people in united adoration of the Father is as necessary to the Christian life as prayer."

Some time ago, I suggested to a Christian man of many years that he ought to find a local church where he and his family could become active. "Oh," he said, "you don't have to be a member of a church to be a Christian."

Technically, he was right. Church membership has little to do with salvation. But in a practical aspect he was wrong. I suggested to him that a man could also cross the ocean without the use of a plane or boat, but I would not recommend it. I reminded him of the sharks he might encounter. The church is surely *God's vehicle* for carrying us through the rough seas of our journey on this earth. My friend, it is a colossal mistake to ignore the church!

You, my Christian friend, need the church and the church needs you!

WHY BE A CHURCH MEMBER?

From time to time I am confronted with excuses from people who will not become involved in the local church. "Church members have so many faults," some say. "There are so many hypocrites in the church." I am sure that this is true! There never was a perfect church, or a perfect Christian, for that matter. Even the first-century churches had their problems. *People with problems* need the church just like sick people need a hospital.

Once a person has received Jesus Christ as personal Savior, he needs to be *built up in the faith*. He needs to receive spiritual instruction and to share with other believers—to have opportunity for *Christian fellowship*. The church, through its ministries, is an instrument of training and provides *an atmosphere for spiritual growth*.

Every Christian needs the church and its people in the dark hours of life. The fellowship of believers forms a vital unity in which there is strength and comfort. How many of God's people, overwhelmed with sorrow, have been undergirded by fellow Christians? Only those who have passed through hard places can say:

> Blest be the tie that binds,
> Our hearts in Christian love;
> The fellowship of kindred minds,
> Is like to that above.
>
> JOHN FAWCETT

Paul expressed his appreciation for the fellowship of other Christians: "I thank my God upon every remembrance of you . . . for your fellowship in the gospel from the first day until now" (Philippians 1:3-5). Yes, you need the church and the church needs you.

It is not enough to attend and contribute. *You* are needed—your godly example, your presence, your prayers, your influence, all that you are—these are needed. The ungodly do not hide their darkness, and we must not hide our light. The church certainly needs *you*.

WHAT IS THE MINISTRY OF THE CHURCH?

The church is to assist its members *to grow* in

every way possible. The church is a nursery to the newborn and a place of worship, education, and training for the mature believer.

It is interesting to observe the characteristics of the first church as presented in Acts 2:41-47. In seventy years those Christians went over mountain peaks and tossing seas to rock the imperial city of Rome with the gospel of Jesus Christ. Acts 2 shows that this church possessed:

1. A saved membership (v. 41)
2. A steadfast membership (v. 42)
3. A sacrificial membership (vv. 44-45)
4. A serving membership (v. 46)
5. A spirit-filled membership (v. 47)

The post apostolic church was equally evangelistic. In the face of bitter persecution, the church marched forward to evangelize. Since we today enjoy *apostolic succession*, may we also experience apostolic success.

The Bible clearly teaches that the program of the church is *world evangelization*. Christ established the church in order to reach a lost world. The mission and ministry of the church are summed up in Christ's command: "Go ye therefore, and teach all nations, baptizing them in the name of the Father, and the Son, and of the Holy Ghost: teaching them to observe all things whatsoever I have commanded you: and, lo, I am with you alway, even unto the end of the world. Amen" (Matthew 28:19-20).

Billions of people are included in this commission. The mission of the church is missions. The last words of Jesus outlined the plan of action for the church: "Ye shall be witnesses unto me both in Jerusalem, and in all Judea, and in Samaria, and unto the uttermost part of the earth" (Acts 1:8). They were to begin at home. Peter and John witnessed the death and resurrection of Christ and, therefore, they answered, "We cannot but speak the things which we have seen and heard" (Acts 4:20).

Today the need is greater than ever before. We, too, must share the gospel, for the charge of Christ is still our commission today. Let us proclaim the gospel in season and out of season, in the highways and the hedges, in public and private, from January to December, every day of every week, every week of every month, every month of every year, till the job is done. The unbreakable promise of Christ is "Lo, I am with you alway, and even unto the end of the world" (Matthew 28:20).

REMINDERS

According to the Word of God, the church is a permanent, divine institution that shall never be destroyed (Matthew 16:18).

One of the problems of the church is that it is made up of people like you and me. The church is a *divine institution*, founded by Jesus, but it is also a *human institution*. It is not a hothouse operating under ideal conditions in a controlled atmosphere. It is an organized group of imperfect saints, all of whom have faults and weaknesses.

The church is a *called-out group of people*—a people separated by God unto Himself.

You and the Church

> "Church attendance is as vital to a disciple as a transfusion of rich, healthy blood to a sick man."
> D. L. MOODY
>
> There never was a perfect church, or a perfect Christian, for that matter.
>
> People with problems need the church just like sick people need a hospital.

QUESTIONS

1. Why is the church important, according to Matthew 16:18 and Ephesians 1:22?
2. What is the church?
3. Explain the difference between the local church and the church universal, according to 1 Corinthians 1:2.
4. List a few reasons why believers should be members of a local group.
5. List five characteristics of the apostolic church as given in Acts 2:41-47.
6. Though the church exists to help believers grow, what is the program of the church concerning the world?
7. How is the relationship between a husband and wife like that of Christ and the church?

12
You and Your Money

All things come of thee, and of thine own have we given thee. . . . O LORD our God, all this store that we have prepared to build thee an house for thine holy name cometh of thine hand, and is all thine own.

1 CHRONICLES 29:14-16

Money reveals where our interests lie; it can direct our attitudes; it ever exposes us to the danger of worshipping it; and it represents value. Money not only talks; "it screams."

LESLIE B. FLYNN

* * *

Is it true that "money talks"? Yes, even in Christian circles!

Many Christians shy away from the subject of money, but Jesus did not. In seventeen of His thirty-seven parables, Jesus dealt with property and man's responsibility for using it wisely.

Let no one think, however, that giving, for the

You and Your Money

Christian, is a mere obligation, a responsibility. On the contrary, it is a joyous privilege. Giving cannot be separated from the gospel. The gospel, in fact, *is* giving. It is in the center of John 3:16: "For God so loved the world, that *he gave* his only begotten Son."

God gave, and we should want to give. This is the core of what the apostle Paul is saying in 2 Corinthians. To challenge, and possibly to shame the Corinthian believers, he tells how believers in Macedonia, in spite of "great trial of affliction" and "deep poverty" (2 Corinthians 8:2) had begged for a share in helping needy Christians at Jerusalem.

Years before, on the Asiatic side of the Aegean Sea, Paul had experienced his Macedonian vision. The call had been, "Come over into Macedonia, and help us" (Acts 16:9).

Now there had been a second call. Not, "Come over and help us," but, "Come over and take our help to others."

For the Macedonian Christians, giving was not a chore but a challenge, not a burden but a blessing. Giving was not something to be avoided, but a privilege to be desired.

The danger for these Macedonians was not that they would give too little, but that they would give too much.

Suffering often produces selfishness, for too often we take special care of ourselves and forget others. Not so with these Christians. They experienced great trials and deep poverty, but this double yoke could not cramp their largeheartedness.

The way they gave is also notable. "And this they

did," says 2 Corinthians 8:5, "not as we hoped, but first gave their own selves to the Lord, and unto us by the will of God."

Notice the sequence. The first step in Christian giving is not your money but *you!* Then sharing what *you have* will follow. The Dead Sea is a dead sea because it continually receives and never gives.

THE TITHE

But some may ask, "What about the tithe?" The tithe, according to the Bible, is one-tenth of a man's possessions. People often dismiss tithing with the casual remark, "We are not under law but grace."

This statement is true, but remember, the Gospel of grace always goes beyond the law. The law declares, "Thou shalt not kill," but the gospel says, "Thou shalt not hate," and even more, "Thou shalt love."

The law of Moses demanded one-seventh of the individual's time and one-tenth of his income for God. That was the minimum. The tithe is the starting place, not the goal. Likewise today, the tithe is a starting place, not the goal. The gospel of grace goes beyond the tithe.

Every new convert will want to do under grace at least what was required under law. Dr. Herschel Hobbs has said, "The nine-tenths prove man's love, but the one-tenth tests man's legal obedience." Make your money immortal: "Lay up for yourselves treasures in heaven" (Matthew 6:20).

Giving should also be *systematic*. First Corinthians 16:2 says, "Upon the first day of the week let every one of you lay by him in store, as God hath prospered him." At the very beginning of your Christian life, acquire the habit of regular giving.

In addition to giving systematically, we should give *cheerfully*. To have part in God's program is a happy privilege. Paul puts it this way in 2 Corinthians 9:7: "Every man according as he purposeth in his heart, so let him give; not grudgingly, or of necessity: for God loveth a cheerful giver."

When we come to the end of life, the question will be, "How much have you given?" not, "How much have you gotten?"

It will be, "How much have you sacrificed?" not, "How much have you saved?" We are to be producers rather than parasites, givers rather than getters.

CHRIST'S EXAMPLE

The *motive* for all Christian giving is summed up beautifully in 2 Corinthians 8:9: "For ye know the grace of our Lord Jesus Christ, that, though he was rich, yet for our sakes he became poor, that ye through his poverty might be rich."

Jesus Christ gave everything. He "emptied himself" (Philippians 2:7, ASV). Four truths are plain. He was rich; we were poor. He became poor; we became rich. Let's think about these great facts for a moment.

1. He was rich.

In the beginning when all was dark, God spoke

and spun all creation into being. God said, "Let there be light" (Genesis 1:3), and the sun was set afire in the skies.

He spangled the night with the beaming moon and shimmering stars. Then, between day and night, He placed the world and started it on its journey around the sun.

Then God scooped out the valleys and bulged up the mountains. God cooled the hot earth with water, dividing the land from the seas. Then the flowers blossomed. Fruit trees produced. Herbs sprouted.

After this, God placed living creatures on the earth—beasts of every kind. "And God saw that it was good" (Genesis 1:25).

Finally, God made man. He breathed into him His breath, and man became a living soul. All creation declares the Creator's might and wisdom.

God is rich in power. All the silver and gold belong to Him. The diamonds in the black caverns of earth are His. The cattle on a thousand hills belong to Him.

He is rich in wisdom. He is omniscient. The past, present, and future are one eternal *now* to Him. He is rich in life. When He came to earth and took the form of man, death had no claim on Him. He is God from everlasting to everlasting.

2. *We are poor.*

How poor are we? So poor that we have nothing with which to plead in heaven's courts. We are so poor that we could not afford a lawyer to plead our case, so poor that we have no robes to cover our guilt and nakedness.

Romans 3 spells out the sorry story: "As it is written, There is none righteous, no, not one . . . there is none that seeketh after God. They are all gone out of the way, they are together become unprofitable; there is none that doeth good, no, not one. Their throat is an open sepulchre; with their tongues they have used deceit; the poison of asps is under their lips: whose mouth is full of cursing and bitterness: their feet are swift to shed blood: destruction and misery are in their ways: and the way of peace have they not known" (vv. 10-17).

We were poor. How poor? So poor that we had no medicine that would cleanse our sin. So poor that we could find no bread or water for our thirsty souls. *We were poor.*

3. *He became poor.*

Jesus Christ is the supreme example of giving: "For your sakes he became poor, that ye through his poverty might be rich" (2 Corinthians 8:9).

How poor did He become? He was so poor that there was no place for Him to be born. He was born in a stable with the cattle as His witnesses.

Think how He could have come. He could have been born in a palace, rocked in a golden cradle, fed with a golden spoon. He could have had angels as His attendants.

But no. As Philippians 2 tells us, He "made himself of no reputation, and took upon him the form of a servant, and was made in the likeness of men: and being found in fashion as a man, he humbled himself, and became obedient unto death, even the death of the cross" (vv. 7-8).

How poor was He? So poor that, even though He

had made the world, He had no place to dwell. The ground was His couch, the rocks His pillow, the brook His wash basin, the breeze His towel, and the wind His comb.

One day He spoke to a multitude, and we read that after He had finished "every man went unto his own house" (John 7:53). But the same gospel narrative goes on to say that "Jesus went unto the mount of Olives" (John 8:1).

When He died, it was as a poor man, crucified between two criminals. He was so poor that He had to commit His mother to another's care. When it was time for the burial, He was not buried in His own tomb but the tomb of another.

Why did He become poor? "For your sakes"— for the sake of those who were lost—for those who were poor. For me. For you.

4. We become rich.

How rich do we become? As rich as Jesus Christ Himself. We were dead—without hope—but now we are alive, children of God. We are not only children, but heirs. We are priests and kings, and we shall reign with Him.

How rich do we become? All the wealth that is His becomes ours. We are joint heirs with God.

Triumphantly we ought to sing:

My Father is rich in houses and lands,
He holdeth the wealth of the world in His hands.
Of rubies and diamonds, of silver and gold,
His coffers are full,
He has riches untold.

HARRIETT E. BUELL

Yes, and these riches are ours, for if we have trusted Christ we can also sing:

I'm a child of the King, a child of the King
With Jesus my Saviour, I'm a child of the King.
HARRIETT E. BUELL

He has made us rich. What shall we give in return? What shall I do with this little life of mine—my money, my time? Shall I withhold it? Dare I withhold it? What will you do?

Remember the grace of our Lord Jesus Christ.

REMINDERS

Money not only talks; it screams.
LESLIE B. FLYNN

In seventeen of His thirty-seven parables, Jesus dealt with property and man's responsibility for using it wisely.

For the Macedonian Christians, giving was not a chore but a challenge, not a burden but a blessing. Giving was not something to be avoided, but a privilege to be desired.

When we come to the end of life, the question will be, "How much have you given?" not, "How much have you gotten?"

Jesus Christ is the supreme Example of giving.

The Dead Sea is a dead sea because it continually receives and never gives.

QUESTIONS

1. Did Jesus speak often of giving?
2. According to 2 Corinthians 8:5, how did the Macedonian Christians give?
3. List two things that should characterize our giving, according to 1 Corinthians 16:2.
4. According to 2 Corinthians 8:9, who is the supreme example of giving?
5. How did Jesus Christ assume our poverty?
6. Share something about our riches as the children of God.

13

Scripture Promises for Spiritual Problems

> *Whereby are given unto us exceeding great and PRECIOUS PROMISES: that by these ye might be partakers of the divine nature, having escaped the corruption that is in the world through lust.*
>
> 2 PETER 1:4

* * *

When you received Jesus Christ as your Savior, you became a member of the family of God. As a child of God, your wealth increased, for you inherited thousands of guaranteed promises. May I encourage you to *read them, believe them,* and *live* in the reality of them.

HELPFUL SUGGESTIONS

1. *Read* these promises from God's Word and memorize as many as possible. I often type them out on note cards and carry them with me

so that I can memorize God's Word whenever I have some unexpected free time.
2. *Accept* these promises as they are. For the most part, do not spiritualize. Someone has said, "Those who spiritualize tell spiritual lies, because they lack spiritual eyes."
3. *Do* your part. If the promise says "repent," then repent. If it says "pray" then pray.
4. *Commit* your life and area of need to the Lord. He is totally trustworthy. The promise may be fulfilled immediately or the answer may be delayed, but the important thing is that we lay our cares at His feet. With Paul we can enthusiastically say, "And being *fully persuaded* that, what he had *promised,* he was able also to *perform*" (Romans 4:21).

Answers to Prayer

"And call upon me in the day of trouble: I will deliver thee, and thou shalt glorify me."
Psalm 50:15

"Evening, and morning, and at noon, will I pray, and cry aloud: and he shall hear my voice."
Psalm 55:17

"Therefore I say unto you, What things soever ye desire, when ye pray, believe that ye receive them, and ye shall have them."
Mark 11:24

"For every one that asketh receiveth; and he that seeketh findeth; and to him that knocketh it shall be opened."
Luke 11:10

"If ye abide in me, and my words abide in you,

ye shall ask what ye will, and it shall be done unto you."

JOHN 15:7

THE BIBLE

"For ever, O LORD, thy word is settled in heaven."
PSALM 119:89

"The grass withereth, the flower fadeth: but the word of our God shall stand for ever."
ISAIAH 40:8

"All scripture is given by inspiration of God, and is profitable for doctrine, for reproof, for correction, for instruction in righteousness."
2 TIMOTHY 3:16

"Thy word is a lamp unto my feet, and a light unto my path."
PSALM 119:105

"Study to shew thyself approved unto God, a workman that needeth not to be ashamed, rightly dividing the word of truth."
2 TIMOTHY 2:15

"So then faith cometh by hearing, and hearing by the word of God."
ROMANS 10:17

CHRIST'S RETURN

"Looking for that blessed hope, and the glorious appearing of the great God and our Saviour Jesus Christ."
TITUS 2:13

"Beloved, now are we the sons of God, and it doth not yet appear what we shall be: but we know that, when he shall appear, we shall be like him; for we shall see him as he is."

1 JOHN 3:2

"Therefore judge nothing before the time, until the Lord come, who both will bring to light the hidden things of darkness, and will make manifest the counsels of the hearts: and then shall every man have praise of God."

1 CORINTHIANS 4:5

"For the Lord himself shall descend from heaven with a shout, with the voice of the archangel, and with the trump of God: and the dead in Christ shall rise first: then we which are alive and remain shall be caught up together with them in the clouds, to meet the Lord in the air: and so shall we ever be with the Lord."

1 THESSALONIANS 4:16-17

CLEANSING

"If we confess our sins, he is faithful and just to forgive us our sins, and to cleanse us from all unrighteousness."

1 JOHN 1:9

"But if we walk in the light, as he is in the light, we have fellowship one with another, and the blood of Jesus Christ his Son cleanseth us from all sin."

1 JOHN 1:7

"But he was wounded for our transgressions, he was bruised for our iniquities: the chastisement of our peace was upon him; and with his stripes we are healed."

ISAIAH 53:3

"And almost all things are by the law purged with blood; and without shedding of blood is no remission."

HEBREWS 9:22

"In whom we have redemption through his blood, the forgiveness of sins, according to the riches of his grace."

EPHESIANS 1:7

ETERNAL LIFE

"For God so loved the world, that he gave his only begotten Son, that whosoever believeth in him should not perish, but have everlasting life."

JOHN 3:16

"Verily, verily, I say unto you, He that heareth my word, and believeth on him that sent me, hath everlasting life, and shall not come into condemnation; but is passed from death unto life."

JOHN 5:24

"My sheep hear my voice, and I know them, and they follow me: and I give unto them eternal life; and they shall never perish, neither shall any man pluck them out of my hand.

JOHN 10:27-28

"These things have I written unto you that believe on the name of the Son of God; that ye may know that ye have eternal life, and that ye may believe on the name of the Son of God."

1 JOHN 5:13

FAMILY

"Train up a child in the way he should go: and

when he is old, he will not depart from it."

PROVERBS 22:6

"And I will give them one heart, and one way, that they may fear me for ever, for the good of them, and of their children after them."

JEREMIAH 32:39

"Honour thy father and mother; which is the first commandment with promise; that it may be well with thee, and thou mayest live long on the earth."

EPHESIANS 6:2-3

"Children, obey your parents in all things: for this is well pleasing unto the Lord."

COLOSSIANS 3:20

FEAR

"Fear thou not; for I am with thee: be not dismayed; for I am thy God: I will strengthen thee; yea, I will help thee; yea, I will uphold thee with the right hand of my righteousness."

ISAIAH 41:10

"And the angel said unto them, Fear not: for, behold, I bring you good tidings of great joy which shall be to all people."

LUKE 2:10

"But straightway Jesus spake unto them, saying, Be of good cheer; it is I; be not afraid."

MATTHEW 14:27

"Brethren, I count not myself to have apprehended: but this one thing I do, forgetting those things which are behind, and reaching forth unto those things which are before."

PHILIPPIANS 3:13

"Not that we are sufficient of ourselves to think any thing as of ourselves; but our sufficiency is of God."

2 CORINTHIANS 3:5

FINANCES

"But my God shall supply all of your need according to his riches in glory by Christ Jesus."

PHILIPPIANS 4:19

"Wherefore, if God so clothe the grass of the field, which to day is, and to morrow is cast into the oven, shall he not much more clothe you, O ye of little faith?"

MATTHEW 6:30

FRUSTRATION

"Commit thy way unto the LORD; trust also in him; and he shall bring it to pass."

PSALM 37:5

"Let us therefore come boldly unto the throne of grace, that we may obtain mercy, and find grace to help in time of need."

HEBREWS 4:16

HEAVEN

"Jesus answered and said unto him, If a man love me, he will keep my words: and my Father will love him, and we will come unto him, and make our abode with him."

JOHN 14:23

"Then we which are alive and remain shall be

caught up together with them in the clouds, to meet the Lord in the air: and so shall we ever be with the Lord."

THESSALONIANS 4:17

"And there shall be no night there; and they need no candle, neither light of the sun; for the Lord God giveth them light: and they shall reign for ever and ever."

REVELATION 22:5

HOLINESS

"If any man defile the temple of God, him shall God destroy; for the temple of God is holy, which temple ye are."

1 CORINTHIANS 3:17

"Wherefore come out from among them, and be ye separate, saith the Lord, and touch not the unclean thing; and I will receive you. And will be a Father unto you, and ye shall be my sons and daughters, saith the Lord Almighty."

2 CORINTHIANS 6:17-18

"Having therefore these promises, dearly beloved, let us cleanse ourselves from all filthiness of the flesh and spirit, perfecting holiness in the fear of God."

2 CORINTHIANS 7:1

HOPE

"For thou art my hope, O Lord GOD: thou art my trust from my youth."

PSALM 71:5

"And the LORD shall help them, and deliver them: he shall deliver them from the wicked, and save them, because they trust in him."

PSALM 37:40

"By whom also we have access by faith into this grace wherein we stand, and rejoice in hope of the glory of God."

ROMANS 5:2

"And hope maketh not ashamed; because the love of God is shed abroad in our hearts by the Holy Ghost which is given unto us."

ROMANS 5:5

HOSPITAL

"Likewise the Spirit also helpeth our infirmities: for we know not what we should pray for as we ought: but the Spirit itself maketh intercession for us with groanings which cannot be uttered."

ROMANS 8:26

"Beloved, I wish above all things that thou mayest prosper and be in health, even as thy soul prospereth."

3 JOHN 2

"He delivereth the poor in his affliction, and openeth their ears in oppression."

JOB 36:15

"Behold, I am the LORD, the God of all flesh: is there any thing too hard for me?"

JEREMIAH 32:27

LONELINESS

"Let your conversation be without covetousness;

and be content with such things as ye have: for he hath said, I will never leave thee, nor forsake thee."

HEBREWS 13:5

"For the LORD will not cast off his people, neither will he forsake his inheritance."

PSALM 94:14

"When my father and my mother forsake me, then the LORD will take me up."

PSALM 27:10

"And he said, My presence shall go with thee, and I will give thee rest."

EXODUS 33:14

NERVOUSNESS

"Peace I leave with you, my peace I give unto you: not as the world giveth, give I unto you. Let not your heart be troubled, neither let it be afraid."

JOHN 14:27

"Have not I commanded thee? Be strong and of a good courage; be not afraid, neither be thou dismayed: for the LORD thy God is with thee withersoever thou goest."

JOSHUA 1:9

"What time I am afraid, I will trust in thee."

PSALM 56:3

PATIENCE

"I waited patiently for the LORD; and he inclined unto me, and heard my cry."

PSALM 40:1

"Be patient therefore, brethren, unto the coming of the Lord. Behold, the husbandman waiteth for the precious fruit of the earth, and hath long patience for it, until he receive the early and latter rain."

JAMES 5:7

"Now the God of patience and consolation grant you to be likeminded one toward another according to Christ Jesus."

ROMANS 15:5

"But they that wait upon the LORD shall renew their strength; they shall mount up with wings as eagles; they shall run, and not be weary; and they shall walk, and not faint."

ISAIAH 40:31

PEACE

"Blessed are the peacemakers: for they shall be called the children of God."

MATTHEW 5:9

"Finally, brethren, farewell. Be perfect, be of good comfort, be of one mind, live in peace; and the God of love and peace shall be with you."

2 CORINTHIANS 13:11

"Behold, how good and how pleasant it is for brethren to dwell together in unity!"

PSALM 133:1

"And the peace of God, which passeth all understanding, shall keep your hearts and minds through Christ Jesus."

PHILIPPIANS 4:7

Persecution

"Blessed are they which are persecuted for righteousness' sake: for theirs is the kingdom of heaven."

MATTHEW 5:10

"If we suffer, we shall also reign with him: if we deny him, he also will deny us."

2 TIMOTHY 2:12

"For our light affliction, which is but for a moment, worketh for us a far more exceeding and eternal weight of glory."

2 CORINTHIANS 4:17

"We are troubled on every side, yet not distressed; we are perplexed, but not in despair; persecuted, but not forsaken; cast down, but not destroyed."

2 CORINTHIANS 4:8-9

Presence

"For the LORD God is a sun and shield: the LORD will give grace and glory: no good thing will he withhold from them that walk uprightly."

PSALM 84:11

"Teaching them to observe all things whatsoever I have commanded you: and, lo, I am with you alway, even unto the end of the world. Amen."

MATTHEW 28:20

"And he said, My presence shall go with thee, and I will give thee rest."

EXODUS 33:14

PRESERVATION

"Now unto him that is able to keep you from falling, and to present you faultless before the presence of his glory with exceeding joy."

JUDE 24

"Who are kept by the power of God through faith unto salvation ready to be revealed in the last time."

1 PETER 1:5

"For I am persuaded, that neither death, nor life, nor angels, nor principalities, nor powers, nor things present, nor things to come, nor height, nor depth, nor any other creature, shall be able to separate us from the love of God, which is in Christ Jesus our Lord."

ROMANS 8:38-39

PROTECTION

"The LORD is my light and my salvation; whom shall I fear? The LORD is the strength of my life; of whom shall I be afraid?"

PSALM 27:1

"And of Benjamin he said, The beloved of the LORD shall dwell in safety by him; and the LORD shall cover him all the day long, and he shall dwell between his shoulders."

DEUTERONOMY 33:12

"God is our refuge and strength, a very present help in trouble."

PSALM 46:1

"For the which cause I also suffer these things: nevertheless I am not ashamed: for I know whom I have believed, and am persuaded that he is able to keep that which I have committed unto him against that day."

2 Timothy 1:12

Resurrection

"In a moment, in the twinkling of an eye, at the last trump: for the trumpet shall sound, and the dead shall be raised incorruptible, and we shall be changed."

1 Corinthians 15:52

"Jesus said unto her, I am the resurrection, and the life: he that believeth in me, though he were dead, yet shall he live."

John 11:25

Sickness

"And his disciples asked him, saying, Master, who did sin, this man, or his parents, that he was born blind? Jesus answered, Neither hath this man sinned, nor his parents: but that the works of God should be made manifest in him."

John 9:2-3

"Likewise the Spirit also helpeth our infirmities: for we know not what we should pray for as we ought: but the Spirit itself maketh intercession for us with groanings which cannot be uttered. And he that searcheth the hearts knoweth what is the mind of the Spirit, because he maketh intercession for the saints according to the will of God."

ROMANS 8:26-27

"For this thing I besought the Lord thrice, that it might depart from me. And he said unto me, My grace is sufficient for thee: for my strength is made perfect in weakness. Most gladly therefore will I rather glory in my infirmities, that the power of Christ may rest upon me."

2 CORINTHIANS 12:8-9

"Is any among you afflicted? Let him pray. Is any merry? Let him sing psalms. Is any sick among you? Let him call for the elders of the church; and let them pray over him, anointing him with oil in the name of the Lord: and the prayer of faith shall save the sick, and the Lord shall raise him up; and if he have committed sins, they shall be forgiven him."

JAMES 5:13-15

SLEEPLESSNESS

"Yet the LORD will command his lovingkindness in the daytime, and in the night his song shall be with me, and my prayer unto the God of my life."

PSALM 42:8

"I laid me down and slept; I awaked; for the LORD sustained me."

PSALM 3:5

"I will both lay me down in peace, and sleep: for thou, LORD, only makest me dwell in safety."

PSALM 4:8

Sorrow

"Behold, he taketh away, who can hinder him? Who will say unto him, What doest thou?"

JOB 9:12

"They that trust in the LORD shall be as mount Zion, which cannot be removed, but abideth for ever."

PSALM 125:1

"But he knoweth the way that I take: when he hath tried me, I shall come forth as gold."

JOB 23:10

Strength

"But ye shall receive power, after that the Holy Ghost is come upon you: and ye shall be witnesses unto me both in Jerusalem, and in all Judea, and in Samaria, and unto the uttermost part of the earth."

ACTS 1:8

"Trust ye in the LORD for ever: for in the LORD JEHOVAH is everlasting strength."

ISAIAH 26:4

"But they that wait upon the LORD shall renew their strength; they shall mount up with wings as eagles; they shall run, and not be weary; and they shall walk, and not faint."

ISAIAH 40:31

"Then he answered and spake unto me, saying, This is the word of the LORD unto Zerubbabel, saying, Not by might, nor by power, but by my spirit, saith the LORD of hosts."

ZECHARIAH 4:6

Scripture Promises for Spiritual Problems

TEMPTATION

"There hath no temptation taken you but such as is common to man: but God is faithful, who will not suffer you to be tempted above that ye are able; but will with the temptation also make a way to escape, that ye may be able to bear it."

1 CORINTHIANS 10:13

"These things I have spoken unto you, that in me ye might have peace. In the world ye shall have tribulation: but be of good cheer; I have overcome the world."

JOHN 16:33

"Submit yourselves therefore to God. Resist the devil, and he will flee from you."

JAMES 4:7

WISDOM

"If any of you lack wisdom, let him ask of God, that giveth to all men liberally, and upbraideth not; and it shall be given him."

JAMES 1:5

"And many people shall go and say, Come ye, and let us go up to the mountain of the LORD, to the house of the God of Jacob; and he will teach us of his ways, and we will walk in his paths: for out of Zion shall go forth the law, and the word of the LORD from Jerusalem."

ISAIAH 2:3

"The fear of the Lord is the beginning of wisdom: and the knowledge of the Holy is understanding."

PROVERBS 9:10

Moody Press, a ministry of the Moody Bible Institute, is designed for education, evangelization, and edification. If we may assist you in knowing more about Christ and the Christian life, please write us without obligation:

Moody Press, c/o MLM, Chicago, Illinois 60610.

Notes

Notes

Notes

Notes

Notes

Notes